ANGELS THREE SIX

Confessions of a Cold War Fighter Pilot

Second Edition

Adrian,
Hope you'll enjoy these stories
from a fighter cockpit. I'll bet
some will bring back memories.
Cheers,
Chuck

By Colonel Chuck Lehman

Published in the United States by:
The Write Place
4310 S. Havana St.
Spokane, Washington 99223

ISBN 0-9788507-9-3

Printed in the U.S.A.

To the one who has truly been the wind beneath my wings for half a century--Marian. She has endured far more than I have during this journey. I know it's harder being on the ground, thinking about loved ones in the air, than it is strapped into a beautiful machine, seemingly above it all. Thank you, my Love. You would have been a great pilot.

To all the intrepid air defenders who gave their all to protect this country from the big attack that never came. Many didn't make it back to home plate, including some of the ones in these stories, but they are not forgotten.

TABLE OF CONTENTS

Acknowledgments

I've received so much wonderful support from so many people that I fear that I'll miss someone in trying to name them. This book could not have come together without the superb editing by Marian, my lovely wife of more than 50 years. Her uncanny eye can spot things that this old fighter pilot would miss in a hundred readings. The book would never have been written at all without her urging and encouragement. Interestingly, now that it's on paper she wonders if I should have been so candid, or should have included some of the more embarrassing stories. I wonder about that too. However confessions are confessions.

The photos in the book are almost all at least four decades old. The amazing restoration and editing by our son, Greg Lehman, owner of Greg Lehman Photography made even the worst of them look good. He doubled as a superb text editor. The cover was designed by Brianna Dauenhauer, a talented graphic designer, and our granddaughter. She was also an inspiration to keep me moving on the manuscript.

FOREWORD

By

Major Gen. Wallace (Wally) Hegg, NDANG RET.

While going through Interceptor School at Moody AFB, I discovered that Duluth AB was scheduled to get the new F-106. Thinking that even if they got delayed, the F-102s they were currently flying sounded good. Both aircraft were single seat, and at that stage of my career I wanted to both fly and operate the radar. Later experiences taught me that having a WSO (Weapons Systems Officer) to share tasks was not all bad.

The weather in Duluth, Minnesota in November 1959 may have been wintry and cold but the reception and hospitality at the 11th FIS made my wife Maxine and I feel very welcome. I was assigned to "A" Flight, the same flight as Chuck Lehman. We both liked outdoor activities, particularly hunting, so we soon became good friends. Being members of the same flight meant we were scheduled for the same events on a daily basis, whether it was flying, alert, ancillary training or even the rare day off.

With the arrival of the F-106, naturally, there was

squadron wide competition to see who could accumulate the most flying time. We all thought Chuck Lehman must have some sort of sky hook as he always got slightly more time out of the same fuel load. He was also better than most at sniveling an aircraft out of the other two flights on their primary flying days.

Chuck was always at the top or close for the most F-106 hours. Chuck Lehman was our Squadron Life Support Officer, a very serious and deadly additional duty. Life Support was always a focus area for every Higher Headquarters Inspection team. Chuck's facility, personnel and equipment were always rated above average. As aviators, that always gave us a warm and fuzzy feeling, and gained Chuck our added respect over and above his flying ability. (His knowledge and understanding of life support equipment served him well later in his career when he was forced to bail out).

When the Cuban Missile Crisis erupted, Chuck and I were two of the four primary alert crews that got the scramble order to disperse. We thought just trusting us to fly multimillion-dollar airplanes was a lot of responsibility. Now they were sending us off in single seat nuclear-loaded airplanes—awesome—things were obviously tense.

Chuck's recall of happenings during those tense days in 1962 brings back many memories. Several humorous incidents that he didn't include were all the deer on the runway at Volk Field when we arrived. Naturally, steely-eyed fighter pilots could take care of that problem. When we got done beating up the patch, all the deer were in the next county—who was going to report our antics—there wasn't even a tower operator. We parked on what we hoped was a level piece of ramp, as there were no crew chiefs to set chocks (the F-106 had no parking brake) or ladders. After dropping to the ground, we used every piece of material we could find to block the wheels. As I walked into the building next to the ramp, the janitor, the only person around, was just answering the phone. I could only hear one side of the conversation but it sounded like some Colonel from Duluth was checking to see if we had arrived. The janitor had just said hello, the Colonel must have said, "What rank are you?" The janitor, now very overwhelmed with all the happenings, held the phone at arms length and screamed, "It's Mister, like when you speak to Mister President". He was very relieved when I said "Why don't you let me take that call." His quiet world would be very rudely interrupted for the next several weeks.

As we now know, calmer heads finally prevailed, and life returned to normal. After leaving Duluth, Chuck went on to have a distinguished career in the Air Force. I left the Air Force in 1963, and joined the North Dakota Air

National Guard. Our paths have since seldom crossed, but we have stayed in distant contact. Chuck always calls when he has made another good shot with his Winchester 264 Magnum. (We both purchased identical rifles at the same time). I have been stuck in the flat lands of ND, while he has roamed some of the prime big game areas, no wonder he can brag. Life isn't always fair.

INTRODUCTION

Despite the seriousness of the air defense fighter mission, there were some lighter moments. With few exceptions, such as "At the Brink", this book focuses on these times when the gravity of the world situation was overshadowed by the exuberance, mega-confidence and questionable judgement of youth.

We were dedicated to protecting the citizens of this great nation from the horrors of a successful strike by the huge Soviet Air Force - dedicated enough to accept the *final* attack on an invading bomber. We knew that if our missiles and rockets failed to stop the threat, we had to take the bomber out by ramming it with our own aircraft. There was little chance to survive that *final* attack.

However, we had great machines to fly. Much of that flying was beyond sight of any human being. It was a bit like turning a very confident guy loose with a Formula One race car on a challenging mountain road with no speed limit, no rules and no one watching. You just know he's going to push it. Couple that with the fact that much of fighter flying is done on the featheredge of human capability and aircraft performance, and I hope you can put these stories into perspective. Some are hairy. Others are humorous. A few are zany. One or two (maybe more) fit more aptly into the "How could I Have Been So Stupid" category.

Each is told exactly as I remember it, except that I don't identify the players—other than myself. The stories are confessions, not exposés. In most cases, the events are so burned into my memory that I can still feel the G forces, the vibrations and the flow of oxygen in my mask. I can smell the smells, hear the sounds, feel the sweat—and the indescribable exhilaration of flying a high performance fighter "on the deck." Six hundred knots at 40,000 feet is mundane. That same speed at 400 feet is exciting. At 40 feet it's mind-blowing.

In a few of the stories, the exact words of the radio transmissions have escaped me. Except where I have a tape or transcript to refresh my memory, I have filled in the quotes as best I can, remaining true to the facts of the story. If there are questions as to the meaning of the flying terms used, such as Angels Three Six (thirty six thousand feet) ,refer to the last chapter of this book; "Radio Speak".

Come, take a ride to Angels Three Six.

F-102 off the coast of Vietnam, 1969

F-106 Vertical peel off.

Photo courtesy of Pat'sWorld F106DeltaDart.com

At The Brink

October 1962 began like most other autumns on the shores of magnificent Lake Superior. Golden birches, brilliant red sumacs, and always-green conifers lolled under cloudless, cobalt blue skies. It was paradise for ruffed grouse hunters, late-season Northern Pike fishermen—and fighter pilots. Duluth provided more than its share of challenging weather, but not in early October.

The 11th Fighter Interceptor Squadron, nicknamed the Red Bulls, was one of dozens of similar outfits that lined the Canadian border and both coasts of the US. Organized as the Air Defense Command, they provided a formidable line of defense against hundreds of long range Soviet bombers poised to attack our cities and bases. The cold war could grow hot in the blink of an eye.

To help counter this threat, the Red Bulls were equipped with the F-106 Delta Dart, or simply the "Six", as we called it. Like the F-101 Voodoo, flown by about half the air defense squadrons, the Six was designed to get off the ground fast, climb fast and cruise fast, so it could intercept and destroy those bombers at any altitude in any weather, far north over Canada. Ground Control Intercept (GCI) radar sites and Semiautomatic Ground Environment (SAGE) sectors directed the fighters to a position where they could take over the attack with their sophisticated MA-1 fire-control system.

A typical scenario went something like this. Each squadron had at least two fighters on 5-minute alert, meaning they could scramble, and be climbing toward any threat within five minutes after the raucous scramble horn sounded. Actual times for the Red Bulls averaged around two and a half minutes. The 5-minute alert birds were armed with radar-guided and heat seeking missiles. Backing them up were several aircraft on 15-minute status, armed with the same missiles, plus nuclear MB-1 air to air rockets. These big white 'Blivets," as we called them, were designed to be fired ahead of an enemy bomber, where they would detonate, causing a huge fireball that would virtually evaporate the threat. Backing the 15-minute birds were several one-hour birds, also nuclear armed.

The rationale behind the system was based on time and distance. If the Soviets (we usually called 'em Russians) attacked, they would come the shortest distance. That was over the Arctic Ocean. They'd be detected by our radars, somewhere in northern Canada or Alaska. GCI or SAGE would scramble the 5-minute birds, to hustle out to positively identify the intruding aircraft and shoot them down. If the Russians launched Intercontinental Ballistic Missiles (ICBM's) at us over the North Pole, some very basic math told us we'd have about 15 minutes to react after the missiles were detected. We'd launch everything that would fly, and disburse to non-target airfields.

The problem in October '62 was that it appeared the Soviets were playing a trump card. Rumors were spreading that they were bringing weapons into Cuba. That would change everything. The flight time of their bombers or missiles would be a tiny fraction of what we were set up to counter—and they'd be coming from the wrong way. Most of our defenses were aimed north.

We would be sitting ducks.

They could streak across the Caribbean, literally on the wave tops, where the radars of the time were nearly worthless. They'd be on top of targets like Miami, and Homestead Air Force Base, or a host of others, before even the 5-minute birds could get to them. If they brought in missiles, their flight time from Cuba to the east and southeast coasts would be so short that our first indication of an attack could be a nuclear detonation on a US city.

It was a nervous time.

At the 11th, we got wind of this early in October. All leaves were cancelled and calls went out to everyone already on leave, or on temporary duty away from the squadron, to return at once. We put more Sixes on 5-minute alert, and loaded every other flyable aircraft with nuclear MB-1's. Security was incredibly tight.

At one point the alert hangars were full and about a dozen 106's were parked on the ramp, armed with nukes. Security police were everywhere. As with any nuclear situation, no single individual could get near this area. Everything was done on a "Two Man Concept." Even with all the clearances, badges and background checks, no unaccompanied person could get near those birds without risking being shot.

Suddenly, we heard the unmistakable drone of a World War II vintage P-51 Mustang. A lone propeller driven fighter was entering our traffic pattern at high speed. Its wings bore faded British or Canadian bullseye insignia. The old warbird rolled into an 80-degree right bank, over the end of the runway. Its pilot flew a tight, close-in pattern as we watched in disbelief. Cop cars took off like a covey of quail toward the runway. This guy was going to land.

He touched down smoothly, with only a puff of white smoke from each tire announcing that he was on the ground. Police vehicles turned onto the runway from every taxiway, but they kept their distance from that huge whirling prop. With fifty or so muzzles pointing at him, the Mustang pilot taxied toward our ramp. The cops were frantic.

About 100 yards from the nearest 106, they got him corralled and forced him to stop. His canopy opened slowly. From a tiny cavity behind the pilot's seat, an orange-clad figure popped up, both hands in the air, waving wildly and smiling.

It was Ron, one of our 106 pilots, already dressed for alert. He'd been on leave in Iowa. When he learned of the recall, he didn't want to drive eight hours and risk missing the fun. He convinced a dentist friend to fly him back to Duluth. We all had a good laugh. The cops reluctantly released the Mustang pilot and we gave him a true fighter pilot's welcome. About an hour later we sent him on his way—much to the relief of the security police.

Early on the morning of October 22nd, one of the airmen in our Combat Alert Center came running, wide-eyed into our ready room. "A Russian MIG just buzzed Miami Airport!" he announced.

Lt. Col. K asked, "Where did you hear that?"

"It was on the radio."

Our squadron Intelligence Officer challenged, "If that were true, we'd have gotten the word through channels." That comment got a chorus of laughs. Even in 1962, the media had ways of knowing what was going on.

"OK, guys," Colonel K warned, "This is probably a hoax. If it's not, we'd better be ready for anything."

We checked our authenticator codes and personal gear for the umpteenth time. I was set up in aircraft 092, on 15-minute nuclear alert status. My aircraft and three others were parked in the secondary alert hangar, about 200 yards from the squadron building. My helmet hung from the optical sight, mounted at the apex of the Six's sharply gabled windscreen. My chute was strapped into the rocket-powered ejection seat. 092 was pre-flighted and fully "cocked", with most of its switches already on. Heavy electrical cables provided instant power. Compressed air at 3,000 PSI was plugged in to spin the big J-75 jet engine to starting RPM.

A buzz of speculation hummed through the squadron. We walked the halls, metal spurs clicking on the heels of our highly polished flying boots. When we strapped in for a scramble (takeoff) the spurs locked onto steel balls at the ends of two cables that retracted into the ejection seat to restrain our legs during an ejection. Our blaze orange flying suits, adorned with several embroidered patches, announced we were "Air Defenders," proud to be flying the fastest, most sophisticated aircraft on earth. The Six had recently set a world speed record for a single engine airplane of 1526 miles per hour. That record still stands. On a crisp October day, the Six could be level at 40,000 feet less than two minutes after brake release.

We were a confident-to-the-point-of-arrogant lot. Yet, on this morning the gravity of the world situation made us uncharacteristically quiet. Our families lived either on base or nearby in Duluth. We knew that any base was a potential target for Soviet bombs or missiles. Although we were superbly confident in what we could do with the 106, we also knew there was no assurance that every intruding Soviet aircraft would be detected and "neutralized" in time. There was, of course, no defense against their ICBM's.

I thought of five-year-old Deyonne and three-year-old Greg, probably just getting up. Marian would be making their breakfast. Maybe she was half-listening to the news. U.S. ships and high-flying U-2 reconnaissance aircraft had by now confirmed Soviet missiles were being unloaded and set up in Cuba. I felt certain the U.S. could not stand by and watch those missiles become operational. On the other hand, it seemed equally certain that a military response on our part to destroy the missles, the ships bringing them in, or the launch sites would precipitate an attack on our cities and bases.

It was shaping up as just the sort of situation the 11th FIS and its scores of sister squadrons had trained to counter—and prayed we'd never have to. Neither side had tipped its hand in this political poker game, but the stakes seemed paralyzingly high.

"Scramble the 15 minute birds! Scramble the 15-minutes birds!"

We all stopped dead at the public address system announcement. "Scramble the nukes?" we mumbled almost in unison. We looked at each other in disbelief. A second later the cheap grey tiles of the main corridor resounded with the clatter of four sets of spurs sprinting toward the flightline door.

My heart was pumping peanut butter, as I raced across the ramp toward bay four. It's huge steel doors were already going up, revealing the swept tail and red bull insignia of aircraft 092. Power carts and air compressors roared to life in a deafening din. My crewchief was just ahead of me, bounding up the boarding ladder to help strap me in. As I climbed the ladder my eye caught the red bordered, white panel that recorded the armament status of 092. It showed four missiles and the Blivet. I was about to take off with a nuke—alone. As far as I knew no one had ever been alone with a nuclear weapon.

We taxied to runway 09. My feet shook violently on the brake pedals when we checked our engines. We took off at three-second intervals and checked in with Duluth SAGE.

"Victor November Zero Five through Zero Eight, climb gate to four zero. Vector 360. Maintain your own separation." That called for a maximum power afterburner climb to 40,000 feet on a northerly heading. We'd stay about a mile in trail, using our radar to keep each other in sight. No one spoke during that two-minute climb. I prayed.

At level off, I checked every function of the fire-control system, except its tie-in with the autopilot. If we were going to war I meant to fly the bird myself. The MA-1 system was capable of flying a complete mission, from wheels-in-the-well (just after takeoff) to 50 feet from the ground before landing. It remained for the pilot to squeeze the trigger, launching whatever armament was selected. 092 appeared ready for the worst. Just before we crossed the Canadian Border, Duluth SAGE broke the silence.

"Victor November Flight, turn port in trail to 265. You'll be recovering at Hector Field."

I guess we all breathed a sigh of relief. It looked like we were just being disbursed to a less likely target. Hector was the municipal airport at Fargo, North Dakota, and home to one of the best squadrons in the Air Defense Command. The 178th FIS, Happy Hooligans were renowned for superior skill and spectacular antics. They were an Air National Guard unit, flying F-89J's. We'd be in good hands with them.

Or so we thought. After landing, we were directed to a remote corner of the field, where we were met by fuel trucks, a few maintenance people and a couple of their senior officers. They cheerfully greeted us and just as cheerfully told us we couldn't stay. It seemed they wanted no part of four more nuclear-armed fighters on their field.

We shrugged it off and launched again. This time SAGE sent us southeast about 300 miles to Volk Field, Wisconsin. Volk was an unoccupied National Guard base. It seemed a bit weird that they were putting us on a deserted field. Our controller brought us down though the weather. He gave us wind speed and direction, the altimeter setting—and turned us loose. We circled the field, looking down at a runway and a few deserted buildings. The control tower was vacant, too.

We landed and parked wingtip to wingtip near the tower. We stood there, discussing how we'd protect the aircraft and weapons with the .38 caliber revolvers we each carried on our survival vests. It seemed probable the Soviets had agents in the U.S., and if this thing got out of hand, four loaded fighters on a lonely rural ramp might be an easy target. We joked about our meager handguns, but it really wasn't funny.

Before long a distinguished looking gentleman in civilian clothes parked his car next to the tower, walked toward us with a broad smile. He was an Army National Guard Colonel. He said he'd get sentries for our aircraft, and that we could use one small ward of the old base hospital as a makeshift alert facility. It had a scramble horn already hooked up to a phone line from the SAGE Sector in nearby Madison. He said fuel trucks would arrive shortly.

"You're probably hungry," he said, "I've got a couple of wonderful ladies, who've volunteered to come out and cook for you. They'll set up the hospital kitchen. Everything should be pretty convenient." Things were looking up.

Within an hour, we were settled into the wooden, World War II era hospital, and got the heat and water turned on. We even found an old black and white television set that would pick up the Madison stations. There were no secure phone lines, so official intelligence reports were out of the question. We'd have to depend on the media to keep us informed on how the conflict unfolded.

In one corner of the ward stood a huge siren, bigger than a garbage can. It was the kind that was usually mounted on a high pole or tower to warn an entire neighborhood. It looked rather intimidating in a single room. We knew that if "the balloon went up," as we referred to the awful day when U.S. and Soviet forces went head to head, that siren would scramble us into the fury.

That's what we were trained for, so we were excited, but deeply concerned for our families. Everyone agreed there would be terrible losses on both sides. Whole cities would be wiped out. Some bases that launched our bombers and defense fighters would not be there when they returned. All of us had families at one of those targets.

Virtually non-stop news bulletins kept us up to date on events surrounding the crisis. One really got our attention. President Kennedy was to address the nation that night. Obviously, any negotiations between the two countries were being conducted in secret, but we felt sure the president would announce what the U.S. would do to defuse the crisis.

The Soviets' Cuban launch sites were rapidly becoming operational. Once those missiles were ready to fire, the Soviets could take out targets in the southeast before we could respond. They'd be in a great position to intimidate. It seemed incomprehensible that the president could allow the missiles to stay in Cuba. Yet, the alternative could mean a pre-emptive strike by the U.S.—and all-out nuclear war.

We paced, watched television and rechecked our aircraft. Well before the president's talk, we were riveted to the screen. Our birds were cocked, on a 5-minute status about 300 yards down the hill, guarded now by ANG security police. We were fully suited up, and prepared for the worst. Outside, a National Guard stationwagon sat waiting to speed us to four gray, delta-winged fighters.

President Kennedy spoke confidently, as he threw down the gauntlet to the Soviet Union. In effect, it was, "Get those missiles out of Cuba, or we go to war."

For a few seconds we sat silently. Then nervous smiles passed among us. None of us really believed the Soviets would back down. Surely, they had considered that potential U.S. response before they made the decision to move ballistic missiles so close to our shores. It looked like war.

I stood up slowly. After taking one last look at the commentators discussing the impact of the president's message, I headed for the old pay phone in the hall. My hands shook as I dialed our house in Duluth. Marian answered. I could hear her folks in the background, playing with the kids. They were visiting from southern Minnesota. I tried to sound calm and assured as I said, "Honey, I can't tell you where I am, but there's something I need you to do for me."

"Sure," she said cheerfully.

"Load your folks and the kids into the station wagon, and drive straight to Blooming Prairie. Don't go through the Cities (Minneapolis/St. Paul). Use the country roads. Just stay at the farm until I call you. I've gotta go. I love you all. See you soon." I wasn't sure of that last comment. Hopefully, they'd get away from one target area and avoid a second. The Amundson farm should be as safe as anywhere. She would have been listening to the president, and would know how important it was to get on the road quickly.

We went to bed early. We wanted to be fresh for whatever the Soviets chose to do. I didn't sleep for several hours, as my mind raced between the situation, my family and what I might have to do with the F-106. Sometime after midnight I dozed off.

At 3:07 AM the ward exploded with unbelievable sound—so loud it hurt. That monstrous siren was screaming. We bolted out of bed, trying to shield our ears, and pull our boots on at the same time. We rushed through the door into the night. This was it!

Snowflakes as big as ping-pong balls filled the air. Visibility was maybe 50 yards, far below takeoff minimums. No matter! Someone said, "They sure picked a great night to hit us." We had to drive slowly down the hill to our birds, so we wouldn't slide into one of them.

I scrambled up the ladder, heart racing. Visions of Russian Bear Bombers streaming south over Canada flashed through my mind. One would be headed toward Duluth. As I grabbed the throttle, ready to slam it outboard to initiate the starting sequence, I looked left, under the canopy rail. Three helmeted faces looked back from their cockpits. They seemed to be in shock. So was I.

A shadowy figure appeared through the snow, running in front of us. He repeatedly swept an outstretched index finger across his throat. It was our squadron commander—

and he was canceling the scramble. He had driven to Volk Field during the night.

The siren had been triggered as melting snow got into its wiring. For the moment, the war was over.

The Soviets eventually backed down. The rest is history," as they say. The two super powers settled back into years of cold war.

F-106 firing the MB-1 Nuclear Air to Air Rocket.
Photo courtesy of Pat'sWorld F106DeltaDart.com

This F-106 awaits it's armament load of four missles and a nuclear rocket.

Faux War

On the wall of a Vietnam latrine, someone had scribbled, "Why do air defense pilots think this war is simulated?" While I don't believe that was true, there was some reason to think it might have been. Air defense fighter pilots lived, studied, flew and trained to win an unending series of simulated wars, staged by the North American Air Defense Command (NORAD) from its nuclear-blast-proof headquarters inside Cheyenne Mountain in Colorado Springs. Several times each year, every squadron had to show that it could perform it's mission of defending the US from an all-out Soviet nuclear bomber attack.

The folks at NORAD did everything in their power to make these tests as realistic as possible. A typical scenario went something like this. Large numbers of aircraft would be covertly staged in Canada to act as the bogeys (bad guys). Once they were in position, a series of simulated intelligence messages would be sent out, indicating a build-up and readying of the Soviet forces. Our response was to put additional aircraft on alert and to perform a mass loading of armament, proving we could get our force ready to fight in a hurry. The intelligence messages continued to show an ever-increasing threat. At some point, a message would indicate the Soviets had launched intercontinental ballistic missiles against the US mainland.

The US was in no position at that time to stop those missiles. We could only try to save our fighter force to counter the bomber attack that was sure to follow a missile launch. Each squadron would "Flush the Fleet," scrambling every fighter interceptor that would fly. Once we were airborne, NORAD controllers would direct us to a predetermined group of airfields that were located away from obvious target areas. Some of these were National Guard bases. Others were civilian airports that were not in major population centers. Sometimes we would fight the "war" from these dispersal bases. Other times we'd return home, after proving we could "Get outta Dodge," in a hurry.

When we got the word that the Soviet bomber force was coming across the Arctic Ocean, and were being tracked by three lines of air defense radars in Canada and the far northern US, we would step up our alert status even more. About the time the simulated "Bad Guys" got within a few hundred miles from the US border, the dozens of bogeys would take off in Canada, and streak toward their "targets" across the US. We would be scrambled again to intercept and "destroy" every one of those bogeys. They would use any evasive action they could, as well as various radar jamming techniques, including dropping bundles of chopped aluminum foil "chaff". They'd also jam our communication with our ground controllers. Couple this with bad weather, or very low altitude bogeys, and the operation got pretty sporty.

Flying a couple hundred feet off the deck in bad weather is a challenge in itself. Doing it with your face pressed against the "muff" that surrounded the radar scope, and catching only fleeting glances at the flight instruments, compounded the problem. Doing both while counteracting the bogey's jamming, evasive action and chaff, created as difficult a situation as any in military flying. The two-place fighter interceptors compensated for that by having an RO (Radar Operator) in the back seat to handle scope and jamming. We didn't have that luxury in the F-102 or 106.

During one of these exercises at Goose Bay, Labrador (N.E. Canada) the bogeys were proving to be a real challenge. Then, in the heat of the battle, a Russian seal harvesting ship captain began shouting instructions on our radio channels to his hunting parties in very broken English. No matter what channel we tried he was always there, preventing our controllers from directing us to the bogeys. It looked like the "bad guys" were going to get through.

Suddenly, one of our jocks broke in, "Shut up, Gary! We know that's you." He had recognized the "Russian's" cleverly disguised voice. It was one of our own pilots who had been drafted to fly one of the bogeys. That's how he was able to follow all our channel changes.

One of the most unusual of these NORAD exercises occurred at Duluth, while I was flying the brand new F-106. We had just transitioned from the F-102 into the 1500-MPH "Six." As dawn broke, it was clear as a bell, with a temperature of minus 31 degrees. When it's that cold, a jet engine has far more power than it does at normal temperatures. Shortly before the order came to flush the fleet, our commander got a phone call from the civilian control tower. They asked if he would accept unrestricted climbs when the order came. Asking a fighter jock a question like that is like asking a kid if he'd like a chocolate bar. As a result, we could climb any way we chose. Maintenance had downloaded all our drop tanks, so we were flying "clean" birds. There was no extra weight or drag from the extra fuel tanks—just a super-slick, new bird that was designed to climb and go fast.

Remember, this was 1960. Retelling it today still seems unreal. On takeoff, I sucked up the landing gear as soon as the weight was off them and stayed in the ground effect (very low over the runway) accelerating quickly in full afterburner. At 400 knots, I pulled up sharply and rolled into a 45 degree left bank. By maintaining that speed and bank angle until the bird reached .92 Mach, I stayed within the field boundaries, and leveled at 45,000 feet, right over the runway—after only 270 degrees of turn and two minutes on the clock. For today's fighters that may seem mundane, but in 1960 it was mind blowing.

The weather in Canada was awful, so someone at NORAD had decided to stage the bogeys in the southern US instead of Canada. As a result, my wingman and I joined up and were directed south to intercept our bogey. We stayed in loose formation as the controller said our bogey was twelve o'clock (straight-ahead) at 60 miles.

"No Joy," (I do not have a radar contact) I answered.

"40 miles."

"20 miles"

"No Joy," I repeated with some annoyance.

"Victor November Flight, your bogey is twelve o'clock at 10 miles, we show him at Angels 40," the controller droned.

I began to doubt the controller's reading of the bogey's altitude. Forty thousand feet below was a sea of white—solid low clouds. There, just above the undercast, was a tiny speck—the B-57 bogey.

"He's low. Follow me," I said to my wingman.

I rolled into a near vertical dive, reducing the power a bit. Still, we accelerated briskly. At some point in the dive I saw 1.87 Mach on the gauge. We made a successful attack on the bogey and headed home, feeling great. However, we were greeted in the fuel pits by a very angry colonel.

"What in the ____ were you trying to do, Lehman?"

"We got the target, Sir," I responded, cautiously.

"Yeah, but how did you get it?"

"The only way we could, Sir. The bogey was almost 40,000 feet below us. Their height-finders must have been way off. We had to dive on the bogey. Is there a problem?" I sensed that he was pleased we had upheld the squadron's reputation, but something was definitely bothering him.

"How fast did you go in that dive?

"I don't know exactly, Sir. Close to Redline (maximum safe speed for the aircraft) I think. I saw 1.87 Mach on the way down"

His forehead furrowed more as he asked, "Where was the bogey when you splashed him?"

I began to suspect the reason for his angst. The Dart created an awesome sonic boom, when it was supersonic. That's why we always flew our Mach one-plus training sorties at 45,000. From that altitude the boom rarely reached the ground. However, we had bottomed out of our dive at about 4,000 feet, still very definitely supersonic. Also, the boom is magnified when the nose of the aircraft is pointed at the ground.

"Oh, oh," I mumbled.

"I'll tell you where you were—at nearly Mach two. You were over downtown Minneapolis. All hell has broken loose down there. Are you sure you got that bogey?"

"We got him, Sir," I said sheepishly, trying to visualize what an aimed sonic boom from TWO aircraft at 1,400 Knots would sound like—or feel like.

His scowl faded. A faint smile showed as he said, "Ah, hell. They'll get over it. Ya done good."

We never heard another word about it. What a guy!

NORAD exercises were not all fun and games. The best intelligence reports of the day said the Soviets would most likely attack in waves, over several days. So, we usually got scrambled two or three times during the first 24 hours. Then we'd get a simulated intelligence report that the bad guys were on the ground, gearing up for another wave. That would temporarily reduce the threat level. Typically, we were pretty beat by that time. The only places to rest were the chairs in the briefing room or the tile floors in the hallways. An hour or two on the tile was OK the first night—but these exercises lasted 72 hours, with usually three scrambles per 24 hours. That last scramble was agony and often came at 2 or 3:00 AM. I can remember running across the ramp for the ninth time, literally stumbling on the ladder, then stepping over the canopy rail, into the cockpit, feeling I was not safe to even taxi the bird. Usually, that was when the weather went Delta Sierra (Dog Sh—). It was a dangerous situation.

NORAD lost some aircraft and a few pilots, but the prevailing wisdom said we should train the way we would fight. That all changed one horrible night when all the squadrons from Wisconsin to Washington were in the late stages of an exercise. The weather went to pot all across the area. Dozens of fighters were low on fuel and all the fields socked in at once. Nine aircraft went down that night.

Shortly thereafter, the exercises were redesigned to allow the crews to get some real rest between waves. None of us missed the old days.

Four "Six's" in Diamond show formation.
Photo courtesy of Pat's World F106DeltaDart.com

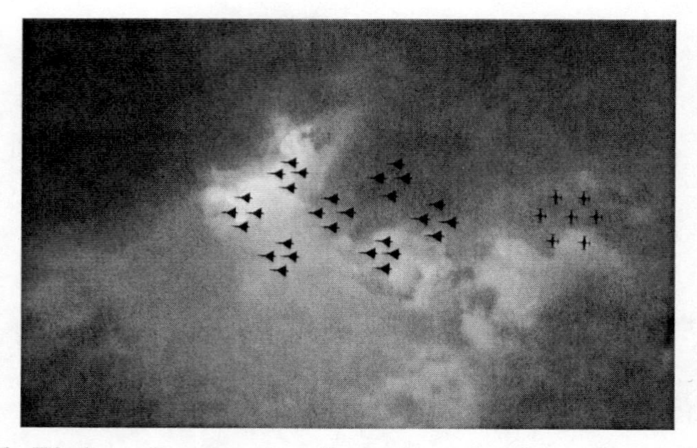

59th Fighter Interceptor Squadron in show formation of F-102's and T-33's over Goose Bay, Labrador

Air Show

There's something about an air show that steps up the pulse, and causes adrenaline to flow in the veins of pilots of high performance aircraft. It's more than just a chance to showoff what you do best. More, even, than a welcome break from the routine. Even flying a fighter can become routine. Maybe it's just the chance to let an audience appreciate the beauty of good formation flying, or precision aerobatics—something like the rush an actor feels when the curtain rises on opening night.

Whatever it is, I felt it when we were invited by the city of Duluth to help dedicate the eastern terminus of the St. Lawrence Seaway in 1961. What added to the excitement was the cast of characters. Our flight of four F-106A Delta Darts in diamond formation would be following the Navy's Blue Angels in their blue and gold F9F's. The terminal was surrounded by a heavily populated area, so no aerobatics would be allowed. We were to follow the Angel's six-ship formation, three miles in trail, one thousand feet above the crowd. Behind us would be a twelve-ship diamond of Minnesota Air National Guard F-89 Scorpions.

Federal, state and local dignitaries were on hand to highlight the long awaited connection of the Great Lakes with the Atlantic Ocean. For decades, ships had plied the lakes with cargos of iron ore and grain, but they couldn't reach foreign ports. The seaway was in many ways the Panama Canal of North America. It opened the mines and farms of the Upper Midwest to a world hungry for bread and steel.

Ray was selected to lead our contingent. Hap would fly right wing. Gary was left wing. I was elated to be flying slot—the position right behind and below Ray. In tight show formation the slot man actually put his six-foot long pitot boom under the leader's tailpipe, and flew high enough to put his vertical fin in lead's engine exhaust. That gave six to eight feet clearance. Ray's wingmen would use similar spacing between their canopies and Ray's wingtips. Since their canopies were roughly forty feet ahead of their own wingtips, the wings of all four aircraft in show diamond overlapped. From the ground—and from the slot—it looked beautiful.

We had briefed all aspects of the mission, especially the many safety concerns. Because of the crowd, there would be no position changes, no tight turns and no tolerance on altitude. With 1,000 feet and the 400 knots airspeed, even an engine failure would allow us to turn away from the city and get over Lake Superior before we ejected. The Federal Aviation Administration had restricted all airspace around Duluth during the show. We would have no other traffic to worry about—or so we thought.

Timing was critical. Everyone had to get off the ground on time to get three formations, totaling twenty two aircraft, joined up and over the port precisely between two distinguished speakers. We started engines. Ray called, "Victor November Blue Flight, check in." There was a long pause, as we waited for Gary to check in as Blue Two. Finally Hap called, "Blue Three, ready to taxi." I checked in, too. We looked toward where Gary was parked, and saw him climbing down the ladder, helmet in hand. He was aborting.

"Blue Four, you'll take my left wing." Ray sounded disappointed. I sure was. I really liked flying the slot. But that radio call probably saved my life.

Ray and I took off in formation, with Hap following twenty seconds behind. He slid into position on Ray's right wing during our first turn. We were now a three ship "V". Ray maneuvered us in behind the Blue Angels, and we heard the guard formation turning behind us.

I was amazed. They had put twelve of their eighteen Scorpions in the air, show-ready. Doing that in 1961 with F-106's would have been like walking across Lake Superior.

The Six was an incredibly complex machine, with virtually everything controlled or operated in some way by the MA-1 System, an early digital computer with hundreds of vacuum tubes. When it worked, it was magnificent. More often, one tube would fail, and the computer would shut down. (We never used the term "Crash")

It was a perfect day for the festivities. Not one cloud marred the deep blue sky over an even bluer lake. With some help from the Duluth SAGE Controllers, the Angels flashed over the crowd exactly on time. Half a minute behind them, we were looking good. Our shiny, silver-gray delta winged birds with bold red stripes and raging bulls on their swept tails, looked like a "V" of "V's" Ray glanced back over his left shoulder at me, then right at Hap. We were tight. Other than a bit of turbulence, everything was perfect.

Although my eyes were riveted on Ray's wingtip, my peripheral vision caught the change in color below from blue to brown as we flashed over the crowd.

"Break!!!" Ray yelled, meaning, "Get Away!". He pulled up violently. I rolled left and up, pulling about six "G's". A yellow wingtip with a red light at the end passed under my right canopy rail about four feet away.

"What the heck was that?" I yelled.

Ray responded, "Bug-smasher!" That term was reserved for any light aircraft. "He seemed to pop up from below us."

"Did we hit him?" Hap asked.

"Don't see how we could have all missed him," Ray answered. "Did either of you feel anything?"

"Blue Two, negative"

"Blue Four, negative."

Somehow that little yellow Piper Cub had pulled up through a close formation of 450-MPH fighters without being hit. But for the grace of God, a lot of people below would have died. A collision would have certainly splintered his aircraft, and brought at least one of us down. The crowd would have been showered with airplane parts and flaming jet fuel. Had I been in the slot, there would have been no escape.

We rejoined far out over the lake, after getting our racing pulses under control, and landed without trying to re-enter the parade.

It's said that Churchill once asked a Battle of Britain fighter pilot what flying was like. The pilot answered, "It's hours of boredom interspersed with moments of stark terror." Sometimes that transition occurs in a thousandth of a second.

We all escaped that "Moment" with our hides intact, but the bug-smasher pilot who caused it by violating FAA Rules, died a few weeks later buzzing the river a few miles from Duluth. He hit some power lines stretched across the river. Some people don't learn quickly.

Marian and the kids were watching from the crowd as our formation passed overhead. They saw the little Piper fly directly into our path. When our formation exploded like a covey of quail, they thought we'd hit him. However, he wobbled a bit and flew off.

The crowd loved it. No one expected a really cool bomb burst around a tiny yellow plane.

Sometimes stark terror lasts only a second or two.

F-106 Tail with 11th Fighter Interceptor colors. That little rudder gave the author a wild ride.

Runaway Rudder

Sometimes, flying's "moments of stark terror" occur so suddenly and end so quickly that there's no time for terror at all, until things have returned to the "boredom" phase. Also, at times those moments get associated with a single other pilot. So it was with Hap and me. Our near miss at the Duluth Seaport dedication (See "Air Show") was the first in a series.

A few months later, we were returning to Duluth in formation from a training mission over northern Ontario. It was an early winter day, with a cold wind blowing off Lake Superior. Our runway was about five miles from the water, and 800 feet above lake-level. Saturated air from the lake tended to condense as wind lifted it up that slope. Dense, low clouds often blanketed the base, when only a few miles away, the sun would be shining. At times the end of the runway nearest the lake would be socked in, below flying minimums, while the other end, only 8,000 feet away was clear. It was a weird place to fly.

That day, both ends of the runway were at field minimums. The cloud ceiling was 200 feet above the ground. Hap was leading. I was tucked in tight on his right wing. We skimmed the stark-white cloud tops toward the base at 350 knots, like a pair of bobsleds on the winter snow. Hap throttled back, and called, "Red Flight, Gear, Now." Our landing gear locked down, as we slowed to 180 knots. Hap checked me as we started down the glide slope into the clouds. All was well. The air was glass-smooth. So was Hap. Flying his wing in the soup was a piece of cake. I maintained about eight feet between my cockpit and his wingtip. About 500 feet above the ground, my aircraft suddenly lurched toward Hap's, rolling and skidding, with no control input from me. In half a heartbeat, I was looking over my instrument panel right at Hap's helmet—only a few feet away.

My aircraft continued to roll toward him, as I slammed the stick into my right thigh, stomped on the right rudder pedal. No response! I jerked the stick into my lap and slapped the throttle into the afterburner position. My nose seemed inches from Hap's head. He was unaware. As my burner lit, providing over 35,000 pound of thrust to my bird, it began to respond to my back-stick pressure. I rolled over Hap's aircraft, loosing sight of him in the soup. A second later, I popped out of the cloud deck, standing on my tail. As quickly as my bird had done its own thing, it returned to my control.

"Red Lead, are you OK?" I called, trying to sound calm, as the delayed adrenaline response hit my consciousness.

"Yeah. What Happened? All I could see was fire. My whole canopy was enveloped in flame." Hap's voice reflected his delayed reaction, too.

"That was my burner. Had to use it to miss you. Guess I had a hard-over rudder. It's OK now. I turned my yaw dampers off. They probably caused it." I explained.

His voice returned to normal, as he called, "Do you want a chase?" He was offering to fly my wing as I tried another approach. I felt one near miss was enough.

"Negative," I replied. "If this thing goes crazy again, it's better I'm alone. Thanks."

He called, "Approach control, this is Red Lead. I'll be landing alone. Two had some control problems."

"Roger, Red Leader. You're cleared to land. Red Two, do you read Duluth approach?"

"Roger, Duluth. I'm on top. Request an ILS (Instrument Landing System) approach."

"Red Two, are you declaring an emergency?"

"Negative. Everything's under control." That wasn't quite true. My heart rate was just a bit faster than a humming bird's, and there was some chance I'd have to change shorts.

At least I didn't get enveloped in a fireball. My tailpipe must have been only a few feet from poor Hap's face when that awesome burner lit, surrounding him with searing flame.

Hap and I began to wonder if we should fly together. The maintenance troops were never able to duplicate the problem or diagnose it. Apparently, it was just a momentary electonic glitch.

F-106 escorting a Soviet Bear Bomber
Photo courtesy of Pat's World F106DeltaDart.com

Scramble

The air defense business in the 60's was deadly serious. The Soviet Union had a huge, well-equipped long-range bomber force, armed with hundreds of nuclear weapons, any one of which could take out a major U.S. city. If they decided to use that force, we could not afford to let even one bomber reach its target.

To deter them, or stop them, the U.S. and Canada formed the North American Air Defense Command (NORAD) linking scores of fighter-interceptor squadrons and dozens of radar sites under a unified command inside Cheyenne Mountain in Colorado Springs. Three long strings of radars stretched across the continent. Far to the north, the Distant Early Warning (DEW) Line had the task of detecting an attack shortly after it was launched. The Mid-Continent Line gave more precise tracking, and picked up any intruders missed in the sub-arctic. The Pine Tree Line ran roughly along the Canadian boarder. First with voice radio, and later by computer- to- computer data-link, controllers positioned our fighters for a killing shot with rockets, radar or infrared guided missiles, or nuclear "blivets."

The system depended on the radars detecting incoming bombers (bogies) as far north as possible. The fighters were designed to get off the ground quickly, climb fast, close on the bogey at high speed, fire, and breakaway for another shot.

The thing that made all this technical stuff work was the scramble.

Across the two nations, every squadron had at least two fully armed birds on five minute alert. When a scramble was ordered, these pilots had to have "wheels in the wells," and be climbing within five minutes of the raucous blast of the scramble horn or klaxon. There's no describing the sound of a klaxon, except to say it tended to rattle your teeth.

When scrambles were called in the dead of night, strange things sometimes happened. All fighters are complex machines, and interceptors were even more so. Getting one airborne and ready to fight that quickly, takes some doing—and no air defense pilot was satisfied with a five minute scramble. Most were much faster than that.

Imagine yourself sound asleep on the second floor, with your flight suit, jacket and boots next to your bed. Outside, snow and sleet are pelting the sheet-metal skin of the alert hangar. Downstairs, your five-minute alert bird is waiting with external power plugged in and the ladder hanging from the canopy rail. Your parachute, helmet, oxygen mask and gloves are in the cockpit. In another room, your crewchief sleeps.

It's 2:17 AM. The Klaxon sounds. You have no idea whether the reason is an airliner off course and violating US airspace, an unknown aircraft that must be visually identified—or war. Your pulse races as you jump into your blaze-orange, fire retardant flight suit, Nomex jacket and zip-up boots. You bolt down the stairs, three at a time, or use the fireman's pole if your squadron has one.

The front and rear hangar doors are opening as you dash toward your bird. The crewchief is sitting on the canopy rail, reaching in to start the engine. Three seconds later, you're stepping into the cockpit, with the engine already winding up to taxi RPM. The crewchief helps you don your parachute (three buckles) seat belt and shoulder harness (three straps into one buckle). You snap your spurs onto cables on the ejection seat, and pull the seat safety pins. Your helmet and oxygen mask hang from the optical sight at the top of the windscreen. You put it on, strap it tight, snap your mask and suck huge gulps of 100% oxygen, as you check all the gages, and get the radar fire-control system up and running.

There's so much adrenaline racing through your veins that your feet are bouncing uncontrollably on the brakes.

You give the crewchief, who's now on the ground, the signal to remove the wheel chocks. Your shaking legs release the brakes and you squirt out of the hangar like a spit watermelon seed.

The taxiway is 200 yards long, and angles at 45 degrees to the takeoff position on the runway. You make that turn, peeling rubber off the tires, and light the afterburner. Your head snaps back as 35,000 pounds of thrust, accelerate you into the black. Three thousand feet down the runway, your bird lifts off, and you pull the nose up to maintain 400 knots. At Angels Four Zero (40,000 feet) you check your watch. It is 2:22. Five minutes have elapsed. You beat the clock by quite a bit. You actually got off the ground in two minutes and twenty-eight seconds.

That's the way it was supposed to happen. However, when you operate that close to the edge of human capability, some strange things can happen.

******

I remember one night when there were four of us on five minute alert. Someone had shut off the red night light in the bedroom, and closed the door. It was totally dark. Our heavy winter flight suits, parkas and bunny boots were stationed along the wall, near the door into the lounge area.

About 3:00 AM the horn blasted us out of bed. It was like waking up in a cave. I instinctively reached for my suit and put it on. A few feet away, Frenchy and Bob were struggling and cussing. Finally, someone found the door handle and yanked it open. There stood Frenchy and Bob, each with a leg in the same flight suit. Mac was on the floor, dazed. The door had hit him in the head as he zipped his boots.

We all got off on time.

******

Some squadrons were equipped with two-place interceptors. A radar operator (RO) sat in back and ran the fire control system.

Scrambles in the very early morning presented a special challenge. Full bladders and fighter aircraft are not a good combination. Paul and his RO, plus another crew got scrambled at four in the morning. As they ran to the stairs, Paul realized he'd never complete the mission without a disaster. He darted into the bathroom. Standing at the urinal, he was conscious of someone watching him. He looked over his shoulder, and there inches behind him were three very sleepy jocks, unaware of where they were.

They were just following their leader.

******

Sometimes we'd scramble, complete the mission, then recover at another base. Weather could dictate such diversions. The one Don flew was pre-planed to give the recovery base people training in refueling our aircraft. When he set up on alert, one of our guys asked him to take a box to the recreation officer at the recovery base. A few hours later, Don scrambled with the box strapped into the back seat.

At 28,000 feet, there was a loud explosion in the cockpit. Don declared an emergency and made a rapid descent to land at home. He expected the aircraft to come apart at any moment. Fire trucks lined the runway. He touched down, popped his drag chute and came to a quick stop. As he unstrapped, a fireman jumped up on the wing, and looked into the rear seat. Don climbed out—and was greeted by the smiling fireman holding a broken box and a blown-out basketball.

Apparently, a fully inflated basketball won't tolerate the reduced atmospheric pressure at altitude.

******

When you're rushing to beat the clock, and literally awash in adrenaline, you can make mistakes. One of our jocks got scrambled late at night, in nasty weather. Just as he leveled off, a series of machinegun-like noises rattled through the aircraft. Thinking the bird was in serious trouble, he checked his parachute straps, preparing to eject. They were snug, but he couldn't find his shoulder straps. He snapped on his flashlight, and found the straps lying across the canopy rail—just where he'd put them when he set the bird up on alert. The canopy held them securely, while the leather-covered ends beat the hell out of the outside of the fuselage.

It was months before he admitted why he came home so quickly, leaving the identification mission to his wingman.

******

Once in a while, a "cocked" aircraft would develop a problem that would be discovered by maintenance people. They would call the pilot to set up in a replacement aircraft. Usually, that presented no problem. Sometimes, things went awry.

Late one winter night, I got scrambled alone to intercept and identify an unknown aircraft over Lake Superior. Thick, low clouds blanketed the black water. Snow squalls kicked up huge waves. My SAGE (Semi-Automatic Ground Environment) controller vectored me toward the bogey and positioned me for an identification pass.

"Victor November Zero One, your bogey is at twelve o'clock (straight ahead) at five miles. He's at Angels two point five (twenty five hundred feet. You have a hundred knot closing speed," he said.

No blip showed on my radarscope, so I replied, "No joy (I have no contact) Are you sure of his altitude?"

"Affirmative, Zero One. My height–finder shows him at two point five. Report Tally Ho (I have the target in sight)"

My scope was blank, except for the usual low altitude clutter, and I was in and out of the clouds, so I'd have a tough time getting a visual on him, even if he had his navigation lights on.

The F-106 I was flying seemed to be running on "automatic rough," as any single engine aircraft does over water—especially cold water. I slowed to 220 knots, and descended to a thousand feet, to give me more time to find this guy, and to give my radar a better angle to pick him up by silhouetting him against the sky. Still, the scope showed nothing.

"Zero One, bogey is at twelve o'clock at one mile"

"No joy."

"Half a mile."

"No joy."

"Zero One, break it off! Come port (left) to two seven zero (west)"

We were both frustrated. He probably thought he was controlling an idiot. I thought he was screwed up. He turned me back toward the target, which was bearing down on Duluth. The second pass was no better than the first. I began to think I was chasing a UFO. The 106 should have had no problem picking up that unidentified aircraft, even if it was a bug-smasher (light aircraft).

I had my face pressed against the fake-fur-edged glare shield that extended from the radarscope, trying to pick up some faint return. There was nothing. Flying instruments at low altitude, while spending 90% of your time glued to a radarscope is dicey at best. I was virtually full time on the scope, desperately trying to see any hint of a radar return and checking my altimeter and heading indicator in millisecond glances.

"Zero One, say your tail number." The controller's frustrated voice was replaced by one of obvious concern.

I was puzzled. "I'm in aircraft 086. Why?"

"We just got a call from maintenance. They say that bird is on a red X."

The hair on my neck stood at attention. A red X in the aircraft's records meant there was a serious safety of flight problem with it. A break in the clouds revealed ominous black water, accented with ice flows and white caps. "A red X?" I replied. "What's the problem?"

"They won't tell me, Zero One. They just said 'get it on the ground.' Come starboard (right) to two three zero (southwest) and climb to Angels two zero (20,000 feet). Home plate (the base) is two three five at ninety miles. Weather is three hundred feet overcast, visibility one half mile in snow. What is your state (how much fuel do you have)"

"I have plenty." I pushed the throttle to full military power. The engine sounded as good as they ever do over water and it felt great to put some space between me and the lake. "What about the bogey?" I asked.

His reply was hesitant, and barely audible. "Uh … We have a problem here. Your bogey is not over the lake. He's near Minneapolis. We just got radio contact with him. He's a Northwest Airlines 707."

Minneapolis is almost opposite the direction I was from Duluth. Somehow the SAGE radar was off by 180 degrees, yet they saw me in my actual position, because they read my transponder signal, not my radar return.

I climbed toward home, wondering when my bird would tell me what was wrong with it. Everything seemed OK. I hoped the problem wasn't something that would prevent a weather approach. It wasn't, and the recovery was uneventful. Aircraft 086 was sick, but not quite life threatening.

It was surely a poor night to chase a target that was 180 degrees and 180 miles from where they thought it was—even in a good aircraft. I learned that someone had found the defect with my bird, but delayed just a bit in waking me up to move to a spare aircraft. The scramble horn beat him to it.

******

Combat scrambles had an added urgency that ramped up the adrenaline flow that was present in all scrambles.

The klaxon sounded at 2320 (11:20 PM) at Da Nang Air Base, Vietnam. The North Vietnamese fighter force had been testing our defenses for weeks, by taking off from Vihn and racing south in flights of four. We'd scramble to intercept them, ready to fire a very special missile, head on. The warhead was a moderate explosive charge inside a coil of chain. When the missile got to predetermined range from the bogey, it detonated, and sent a 150 foot chain whirling toward the enemy at three times the speed of sound—a giant chain saw in the sky. It was an awesome weapon. Apparently the bad guys knew that, because they always turned tail and ran back to North Vietnam before we got in range. Rules of engagement at that time forbid us to chase them across the border.

I expected this scramble to be more of the same. Instead, we were vectored over Laos to escort a cell of three B-52 bombers. We called them BUFF's, because they were Big Ugly Friendly Fellas. The BUFF's were going to drop 306 five hundred-pound bombs on targets along the infamous Ho Chi Mihn Trail. Two of us in F-102's were to provide fighter cover for them, in case the North Vietnamese MIG fighters decide to try and stop them.

Earlier in the week, we'd had an intelligence briefing, which warned us that the bad guys had moved some 100-millimeter anti-aircraft guns into the area. They were supposedly capable of downing aircraft at 40,000 feet. The BUFF's were at 37,000, due to their heavy bomb loads. We would stack a bit high and slightly behind them, but we'd all still be in range of the guns. No one considered the guns a major threat—just one more thing to think about.

For us, the ubiquitous Southeast Asia thunderstorms were more intimidating. The F-102 "Deuce" had a strange habit of flaming out if its engine inhaled a gulp of ice crystals. Clouds near the tops of thunderstorms are made of ice crystals.

We slid in behind the BUFF's and S'd back and forth, trying to avoid the storms, while we searched for radar blips that might be enemy fighters. The bomber pilots seemed to like those eight-mile high storms. As the BUFF's flew into yet another thunderstorm, I leaned forward, closer to my radarscope to scan for intruders. The bomber created huge blips that were easy to follow, but a MIG head on was going to be a tiny speck. Constant lightning strobed through the clouds, messing up my night vision.

BLAP! Something that felt like a 2X4 hit the back of my head. My ears rang and I shook my head, trying to clear it. A few seconds later, it happened again on the left side. I scanned the gages and warning lights. Everything was normal. I felt the back of my helmet. It was intact. My cockpit pressure was a bit weak, but not enough to indicate a major leak from shrapnel. I could find no evidence of damage, other than two hard knocks on the head. I didn't want to say anything, because if the bird were truly undamaged, I'd never live it down.

We completed the mission, and landed at Da Nang. Safely inside the alert hangar, I removed my helmet, and checked it. The fiberglass shell showed no damage. However, the inside had two mushy spots, under the leather liner. I peeled the leather loose, and something like snow poured out.

Styrofoam? It couldn't be. My helmet was a test model with a custom fit liner. A foaming chemical had literally been poured in place, on my head. The chemical cured into a foam liner that fit like my own skin. The liner was then covered with glove-soft leather. The foam was supposed to cure with open cells, like a rather firm car wash sponge, so the dramatic pressure changes of flying would not effect it. Somehow part of my liner cured with closed cells. It could not vent pressure as I climbed. Instead, the trapped air finally exploded part of the liner. Two mini-explosions, confined inside a fiberglass shell, felt like something quite different.

I had a quiet laugh—and told no one. There's an old saying in the fighter world, "Never admit you stole the church, even if the steeple is sticking out your rear."

The author in an early partial pressure suit.

Under Pressure

The higher you fly the lower the atmospheric pressure. Our bodies need a set amount of pressure to function. More accurately, they need a minimum pressure of oxygen. Sometimes, the other gasses in the air are a problem. In airliners, designers provide the oxygen by pressurizing the cabin. Fighter designers do the same, but to a lesser extent. A fighter cockpit is so small that any damage (like loosing the canopy) will dump that pressure in a few thousandths of a second. That would do really bad things to the pilot. So fighter cockpit pressures are lower.

Fighter pilots breathe supplemental oxygen through the mask attached to their helmet. Usually, it's mixed with air. In the F-102 and 106, however, we had to fly higher than most others, so we breathed pure oxygen under slight pressure, from the ground up. That was to prevent the

Full pressure suit... better, but not fun to fly in.

bends. Yup, that deep-diver's malady is just as much a problem for high altitude flyers. The reason is nitrogen, that other main gas in air. At low pressures, it tends to boil out of your blood. Bubbles in a cooking pot are OK, but in your blood vessels they hurt like heck and really screw you up. Breathe pure oxygen, with enough pressure to keep any air from seeping into your mask, and the problem is solved—up to a point.

As we climbed, the oxygen pressure in our masks continued to rise. At about 50,000 feet, a pilot could not exhale against the oxygen rushing in. So a loss of cockpit pressure above that would be fatal. In addition, at about 62,000 feet the boiling point for human blood is 98.6 degrees. If you are above that altitude and loose cockpit pressure, you're dead in an instant. Enter, the pressure suit.

Early partial pressure suits balanced the force of the breathing oxygen against the lungs, with mechanical force on the whole body from a tight-fitting suit. They literally squeezed you to help you exhale and to prevent the bends. Tubes, called capstans, along the arms, legs and torso were filled with air as cockpit pressure decreased. That made the suit get ever tighter. The result was good protection—and virtually NO mobility. It was very difficult to move. Just operating the stick, rudders and throttle were a challenge. In addition, visibility through the faceplate was limited to straight ahead. The helmet did not turn. Flying a fighter without being able to look around is a bit disconcerting. To make matters worse, the narrow faceplate would fog up. It had heating wires, like those in the rear window of your car—but turning on the heat to dissipate the fog, caused the plate to distort your vision.

We were required to fly in the suit at least twice a month. We used every excuse to avoid doing it. "The weather's too bad. It's too hot. It's too cold....." Fighter pilots are not known for avoiding a challenge—but we avoided that one.

By the time the F-106 came along, the partial pressure suits were scrapped in favor of newly designed full pressure suits. They were basically a strong, airtight suit with gloves and helmet that actually rotated on ball bearings. They also had a wide faceplate. We could move (some) and we could see, but we still hated them. They were pressurized and cooled with oxygen from a tank of liquid oxygen in the aircraft. They were the forerunners of the suits we see on the astronauts today. Theirs are white for reflection. Ours were orange, like our flight suits, to make us easier to see on the ground after an ejection.

I still would not like to spend more than two hours in any pressure suit. Sorry 'bout that.

Unknown to the author, aircraft 477 (on the right wing) had a reputation.

Out Of Here

Goose Bay wasn't a bad place, even in December. In fact, it was quite beautiful. I'd had to leave Marian behind in Duluth, when the assignment came for "The Goose." That hurt. The base housing officer said there was little chance a house would be available for at least six months. There were none off base.

I was pleased with the 59th Fighter Interceptor Squadron, the famous "Black Watch" outfit. It was a super-squadron, with 36 F102A "Deuces," instead of the usual 18. All the 59th pilots were experienced "Deuce" drivers. I'd been flying F-106's for the past couple of years, so my first two weeks in the squadron were spent transitioning back from the 1500 mile per hour "Six" to the 800-mile per hour Deuce. It was similar to reverting from a 700 horsepower NASCAR to a vintage MG. The checkout went well and I was scheduled for my final check ride early on the morning of 13 December 1962.

I was slated to fly aircraft number 477; call sign Hotel Lima Zero Six. Doug was to be my evaluator, flying another Deuce, call sign Hotel Lima Zero Seven. Both aircraft would be coming off air defense alert status, so they were fully armed with three radar-guided missiles, three infrared-guided missiles and twenty-four 2.75 inch diameter rockets. I saw no significance in being assigned aircraft 477.

Doug briefed me that we were to intercept a T-33 target aircraft (bogey) at low altitude, somewhere north of The Goose. Half Pint, our ground-control site would direct us into position to "attack the bogey". A low altitude bogey at the 59th meant just that.

In two weeks of training, I'd already run intercepts on targets skimming over the trees at 200 feet or less. That made picking them up on the Deuce's radar, amid all the ground clutter, very challenging—especially if you were in the weather. Flying instruments and operating the radar at that altitude was as tough a workload as a pilot gets. To make it sportier, you had to get below your target, so the radar could look up, eliminating some of the ground clutter. Clearly, Doug was going to make sure I could handle any Soviet bomber that tried to sneak toward a US city on the deck.

Our aircraft were in adjoining bays in the four-bay alert hangar at the take-off end of runway 27. The crew chief helped me strap into 477, and removed the ladder. The old reliable J-57 jet engine howled to life. I checked everything in the cockpit, especially the radar fire-control system. Everything was normal.

I glanced back toward the left wing and was startled to see a small stream of jet fuel spewing out of the drop tank on that wing, hitting the hangar floor about ten feet away. I momentarily thought Doug had rigged it as part of my test. That seemed unlikely and the leak posed no threat, so I chose to ignore it. At my hand-signal the crew chief removed the wheel chocks. I called Doug, "Hotel Lima Zero Seven, this is Zero Six. How do you read?"

"Zero Seven reads you five square (loud and clear). I'm ready to taxi."

We switched to tower frequency, and were cleared for taxi and take-off, using the high-speed taxiway that connected the alert hangar to the runway. It merged with the runway at 45 degrees. I shoved the throttle forward, raising a huge cloud of snow behind the hangar. As 477 accelerated, I checked the engine instruments. By the time I merged onto the runway, I was rolling about 40 knots. Judging that speed was critical, because the surface was covered with ice and snow.

It was 21 degrees below zero on the runway, as I lit the afterburner. The Deuce accelerated briskly. I always liked flying in cold weather; because of the big increase in power that cold air gives a jet engine.

Doug rolled three seconds behind me. He was considered a chase pilot, not a wingman, so I didn't have to warn him when I came out of burner. We contacted

Half Pint as we turned north. Thankfully, the weather was great—not a cloud in sight. It looked like this mission was going to be a piece of cake. That was not to be.

Half Pint directed me into position eight miles behind and slightly to the left of the bogey. "Zero Six, your bogey is at one o 'clock (slightly right of directly ahead) at seven miles, now. I have only intermittent radar contact, so he must be low." That was no surprise. I descended to about 100 feet, trying to keep one eye on the rolling hills of northern Labrador, one on the radarscope and one on the instruments, or so it felt. My air speed was 420 knots. "Half Pint," I called, "Zero Six, no joy." (I have no radar contact on the target)

"Roger, Zero Six. He's now twelve o 'clock five miles."

A faint blip appeared on my radarscope amid all the garbage caused by ground clutter. After a couple of tries, I got the radar to lock onto it. That let the computer figure the perfect attack geometry for my missiles. "Judy!" I called triumphantly, announcing that I was taking over the attack. I pushed the throttle forward and felt the push of the engine eating frigid air.

Since 477 was fully armed, I checked the armament switch at least a dozen times to make sure it was in the SAFE position. Those missiles had to stay in the armament bay. This was a simulated attack. At two miles from the target, I squeezed the trigger on my control stick, and waited for the computer to 'fire" when the range was perfect. I maneuvered to keep the aiming dot centered in a circle on the scope. When the missile launch signal appeared, I broke hard to the left and started to climb. It was a perfect intercept on a difficult target. "Half Pint. Zero Six, MA." (mission accomplished), I announced.

I was elated—until I caught a yellow light on the right console. OIL PRESSURE LOW! Oil lights were not uncommon in the Deuce, and they were usually false. I called to Doug, "Zero Seven, Zero Six has an oil light. I'm heading for Home Plate (The Goose). You may as well stay with the target, and get some more intercepts." I saw no reason for him to follow me home. I headed south, and climbed. At 10,000 feet the AC electrical system quit. The AC generator was run by oil pressure. The light was real.

"Zero Seven, guess you'd better join up on me. My AC just failed.

"Roger, Zero Six, I'm on my way."

By the time he slid into position on my left wing, I was at 18,000 feet using about 83% power, to ease the load on the engine.

Doug asked, "Zero Six, do you have any indication of fire?"

"Negative. Why?"

"Well, you've got flame coming out the side of your fuselage, right by the large numbers."

That would be near the front of the engine, where its huge compressor was turning at about 12,000 RPM. I checked everything again. Still, there was nothing but that yellow light. Everything else was normal. Then I heard or felt a faint grinding. It increased rapidly. The oil-starved bearings were starting to melt down. We learned later that the fire Doug saw was really molten metal running back along the fuselage.

"Zero Six is starting to get some vibration. I'm going to throttle back some more, and punch off the tanks," I called. Maybe reducing the drag by getting rid of a 360 gallon fuel tank under each wing would allow me to limp back to The Goose. It was 70 miles away on the southern horizon. I pressed the tank jettison button, and felt two quick thumps as explosive charges blew the tanks off my wings.

"They're both clear," Doug confirmed.

"Half Pint," I called, "How about alerting the Duck Butt." (An amphibious rescue aircraft)

"Duck Butt is already airborne," he replied.

Things deteriorated rapidly. Noise and vibration increased, even though I was constantly reducing the RPM to keep the engine intact. There was no possibility of reaching The Goose. I was losing altitude. At 11,000 feet, I called to Doug, who was really hugging my left wing. "Zero Seven, you'd better move out a bit. I'm going to blow the canopy." He eased away a few feet, and I let go of the stick, and jerked up hard on the seat's armrests. Nothing happened.

The rail over the pilot's head made through-the-canopy ejection impossible.

I thought of the aluminum beam that divided the canopy, three inches above my head. If that canopy didn't go, I couldn't eject. Then I saw it. Near my right knee, a red streamer hung from a safety pin in the armrest. I'd forgotten to remove it during my preflight inspection. I humbly removed the pin, and dropped it on the cockpit floor.

"Doug, I'm going to eject." I tried to sound calm. Actually, I was relieved. What had concerned me most was that 477 would take me almost home, and then quit when I was too low to eject, or that I might hesitate until I was too low for the rather primitive ejection seat to get me out safely. Now that decision was made— with 10,000 feet of air under me to open the chute.

I pulled the armrest handles again, and another small charge sent the canopy careening away. A contrail streamed back from the windscreen, replacing the canopy with milky ice crystals. The hood of my parka was wadded behind my head, preventing me from forcing my helmet back against the headrest to protect my neck. Under the seat a 37-millimeter canon shell lay waiting. When I squeezed the ejection triggers, it went off.

My first sensation was a huge kick in the rear. Then I saw the knees of my orange flying suit come rushing toward my ears. Actually, I learned later that, because of my parka, the tremendous acceleration forced my head down between my knees.

Then I was tumbling through the air, still in the seat. White snow, green sub-arctic firs and blue-sky kaleidoscoped about me.

The lap belt charge fired, releasing me from the seat. Tumbling slowed, and I looked toward my feet, silhouetted against the sky. One of the shoulder straps had wrapped around my right boot. I was falling upside-down with a 200-pound seat tied to my foot. Behind me, I could hear the parachute deploying. Its 28 nylon shroud lines were stowed in the pack by heavy rubber bands. I clearly heard them snapping one by one. When the 28-foot diameter chute filled with air, that seat was going to get me. I kicked violently at it, once, twice, three times. It spun away, just as the chute yanked me upright. My head was forced down, so I could only see the ground, far below my boots. I couldn't look up to check my chute.

Suddenly, I was whirled around several times, and my head was released. The chute's riser straps had been twisted behind my head. I looked up. Panels of brown, orange and white nylon billowed beautifully above my head. Below were miles of snow-covered fir trees and dozens of frozen lakes. Visibility must have been 200 miles. Off to the south, 477 was gliding toward home—with Doug still flying formation with it.

I had to laugh. "Come on, Doug. I'm over here," I said to no one in particular. He broke away from the pilotless Deuce and circled me. I did jumping jacks in the air to show him that nothing was broken.

A few days before, we had been briefed by the rescue guys that the short range of their H-19 helicopters limited their search range to 50 miles from The Goose. I knew I was considerably beyond that, so as I floated down, I looked for a good place to hole up for a few days while a dog team made its way to pick me up. My seat-pack survival kit contained a pretty good sleeping bag, that along with my quilted underwear, winter flying suit, parka, cap and the fleece-backed "nose wiper" mittens tucked inside the suit would keep me warm. It was approximately MINUS 25 degrees on the ground. I'd have to dig a snow cave, but that was no problem. The kit also held a two-way radio, matches, snow saw and the usual array of small survival items. I actually looked forward to a few days in the far-north woods.

At about 5,000 feet I pulled the yellow handle near my right hip, and watched the fiberglass survival kit fall to the end of its 25 foot lanyard—and keep right on going. The lanyard broke. I stared in disbelief as my kit tumbled toward the woods. My winter camping trip didn't look so attractive now.

Before long the trees rushed up and I settled chest-deep into the snow. My chute draped over three trees, making a perfect signal.

Doug buzzed me at treetop level, shattering the incredible stillness. As he pulled up, I heard reciprocating engines. The Duck Butt was coming on-scene. They carried a *real* survival kit—a big red sled, filled with everything I could ever use. Surely, they'd drop it to me. The big, white SA-16 Albatross slowly circled me. Its jump door was open. Standing in the door with his hands gripping the frame was a PJ (Pararescue Specialist). He was ready to jump. I was alarmed. All I wanted was that red sled. If he jumped and got hurt, or hung up in a tree, we were both in trouble. I tried to wave him off holding the empty lanyard in my hand, hoping someone would figure out what I needed.

The Duck Butt made another pass, dropping a smoke flare to check the wind for their jumper. It landed about 50 yards away. A second flare disappeared into the snow only 50 feet away. The third almost hit me. Again, I tried to wave them off. As the sound of the Duck Butt's big Pratt and Whitney engines faded to the north, it was replaced by the unmistakable drumming of a helicopter.

I stared toward the sound in disbelief. "They told us they could only search out to 50 miles," I thought. Never, did I consider that if they had a survivor pinpointed, they would go much farther. The chopper settled into a hover, and its hoist operator began lowering a yellow "horse collar" to pluck me from the woods. Swirling snow, whipped up by his rotor-wash made it hard to see. When I struggled forward a few yards to grab the collar, the chopper pulled up and away. It seemed he flew about a half-mile. Then I heard his engine wind down to idle. He had landed.

"O.K." I thought, "He wants me to come to him." About 20 yards was all I could move through that chest deep powder, before I was gasping for air. I stood there, feeling the sweat welling under my helmet. There was no way I'd get to him. For the first time, I was dejected.

After a few minutes, his engine wound up and he was soon hovering over me again. I stuck my head and shoulders through the horse collar, adjusted it under my armpits and crossed my arms in front of me, facing the cable. The hoist operator winched me up and pulled me inside. He tried to put me on a stretcher, but I pushed him away and picked up a headset to talk to the pilot. "Hey, I'm sorry I couldn't get to you when you landed. I just couldn't move. There must be ten feet of snow down there."

He laughed. "No, no. We didn't want you to come to us. We were having flight control problems and landed to bleed the air out of our hydraulic system."

"Oh, great! If I'd known that you wouldn't have gotten me into that horse collar. Anyway, thanks for the lift."

Twenty minutes later, I was dropped off at the Goose hospital for a routine after-accident physical. From there, I walked to the barber shop to get spiffied up for the inevitable accident investigation board. I knew I'd be testifying before them very soon. From there I walked to the squadron to get on the afternoon flying schedule. The squadron commander wouldn't let me fly. Bummer.

EPILOGUE:

Time really slows down in a tight situation. The total time from the seat firing to the chute being fully open was about two seconds. Yet I could hear those rubber bands snapping one by one in the chute-pack behind me, and had time to kick three times at the seat. Wouldn't it be nice if our brains could operate like that in less hairy situations?

During my physical, the doctor asked if I'd like to call Marian back in Duluth. I considered it, then declined. I was fine, there were no news media at Goose and I knew it was going to be a busy afternoon. BIG MISTAKE!

That Duck Butt was circling over me within 20 minutes of the chute opening. About the same time, a local radio station in Duluth announced, "Captain Chuck Lehman, formerly of the 11th Fighter Interceptor Squadron, here in Duluth, is missing somewhere north of Goose Bay Labrador. Captain Lehman apparently ejected from his crippled Air Force F-102 Delta Dagger (the Deuce's official nickname) aircraft about 5:30 Duluth Time this morning."

I was invited to the commander's house for dinner that night. He offered to let me use his official "free" phone to call Marian. By then, she'd had a very rough day not knowing if I was dead or alive.

The following morning, Rocky, our squadron safety officer, asked me to accompany him, the sector commander and five members of the accident investigation board to the crash site. I jumped at the chance. If there was anything left of 477, I wanted to get some of my gear from the cockpit.

A large commercial helicopter flew us to the area, and dropped us off on a frozen lake about a third of a mile from the site. Rocky and I were in great shape, so we donned snowshoes and got to the aircraft ahead of the others. It was broken into five major pieces. There had been no fire. My checklist, navigational charts and my Russian-style fur cap were still in the cockpit, which was still somewhat intact, except for the floor.

The aircraft had made a perfect landing, shedding minor parts as it glided through the trees. It touched down in a creek bed full of large boulders. Also in the cockpit were the maintenance forms on which the pilot annotates any problems with the aircraft. I picked them up and checked to make sure Rocky wasn't watching. He was back in the trees looking at a live missile that protruded from the snow. I opened the forms and wrote the bird up for a "hard landing." Another big mistake! Those forms were official evidence for the accident board. They were not amused.

The five board members got lots of pictures and copious notes. An hour before sunset a chopper landed to pick us up. It was too small. The commercial chopper had broken down, so the little H-19 that had rescued me was sent in its place. "Sorry, guys," the pilot announced,

"We can only take four of you. We'll come back for the other two. Rocky and I were lowest ranking, so we stayed.

We watched a magnificent arctic sunset, and felt the temperature drop in the afterglow. It was 20 to 30 below zero. I started to laugh. Rocky looked at me and asked, "What's wrong with you?"

"This is crazy, " I replied, "I bail out of a sick airplane in the middle of nowhere, but get picked up in half an hour. Now, a day later, you and I are stuck on a frozen lake, miles from home, with no survival gear what-so-ever. It's going to be a cold night."

"Yeah, I've been thinking about that. How are you at digging snow caves."

We were resigned to our fate when we heard the H-19. He had enough light to land, but we flew home in the dark.

That night the final episode unfolded. I was walking out of the officers club with Minor and Gil, when a beautiful woman I'd never seen before, ran up and locked her arms around my neck. She cooed, "Thank you, thank you for getting rid of 477. That airplane has tried to kill my husband three different times."

Some airplanes are like that.

Aircraft 477 ended up in five big pieces, including the cockpit

The author 1960 with F-106 #087 before it got its nose art.

The author in 1960 with F-106 #087 "The Toothless Tiger". Most pilots in the 11th painted the noses of their birds. Unfortunately #087 crashed not long after this photo was taken.

The author returning from a scramble in Vietnam.

11th Fighter Interceptor Squadron
Christmas card. F-102's

The F-106 without droptanks.
Pilot in partial pressure suit.

Inverted Wingman

In many ways, The Goose was an unspoiled paradise. We were surrounded by thousands of square miles of virgin natural beauty—and we had a magic carpet to help us enjoy it all.

From Ungava Bay on the north to the Straits of Belle Isle on the south, most of Labrador was (and is) a roadless wilderness with no hint that man has impacted it in any serious way. Tens of thousands of glacially dug lakes, filled with ravenous three-pound brook trout and aggressive northern pike, glowed golden in the sub-arctic sunsets. The mighty Churchill River carved it's way eastward from thundering, 200 foot high Labrador Falls along the Quebec border down to Goose Bay and massive Lake Melville, before disappearing into the Labrador Sea. Along its several hundred-mile plunge, dozens of rapids and cataracts churned its sparkling, tea colored waters. Herds of nearly white woodland caribou migrated across the multi-colored tundra and sub-alpine fir forests. Silvery Atlantic salmon crowded countless rivers and streams during their spawning runs. Squadrons of ducks and geese patrolled the vast lands between The Goose and Labrador's spectacular rocky coast.

The Deuce was wonderful for an outdoorsman, and the land was so vast that we could fly for hundreds of miles without being seen by anyone. About half a dozen of the 54 pilots in the 59th squadron took full advantage of the opportunity. With an area that big to explore, there should have been plenty of room. That was not always the case.

One June morning, about a week after ice-out on the lakes, I flew a training mission against a British Vulcan bomber, which was inbound from the U.K. to Goose at 55,000 feet. We were required to wear pressure suits any time we flew above 50,000, and I wasn't wearing one. The only way to get this guy, who was imitating a Soviet bomber, was to attack him head-on, and snap up from below.

GCI (ground controlled intercept) controllers guided me into a position twenty miles ahead of him at Angels 35 (35,000 feet) at 1.2 Mach (1.2 times the speed of sound). We were closing on each other at roughly 1,400 MPH. I locked on to him with my radar and flew the steering dot on my scope to a point six miles from him. The dot then jumped to the top of the scope. I followed it into a steep climb and "fired" three Falcon radar guided missiles.

"Half Pint, Hotel Lima Zero Six has an MA" (mission accomplished)

“Roger, Zero Six. Come port to 195 for RTB.” (Return to base)

“Negative, Half Pint.” I replied. “I’m going to tower frequency. Thanks for the intercept.” It was a perfect day to check out salmon runs. No need to bother the tower with a detail like that. I headed southwest, descending to 500 feet.

Several rivers ran through lush green valleys, flanked by low, tree-covered hills. They were far enough west of The Goose to be well away from any normal air traffic. By flying in the valleys, I could stay out of ground radar coverage, so no one would guess what I was up to. I settled in at about 200 feet above one of the rivers and followed its meandering course upstream. Continuous curves kept me in a series of 30 to 45 degree banks, back and forth—perfect for checking out the water below.

There were a few salmon working their way to the creeks, but not enough to provide much excitement. No moose waded the ponds along the river, either. Somewhat disappointed, I banked right and climbed over a low range of hills, skimming 150 feet over the crest. Suddenly my left wing dropped. I rolled level to check things out. The aircraft didn’t feel right. I craned my neck to look back at my left wingtip. There, eight feet away was another Deuce in close formation—but he was inverted.

He was doing a great job, despite the trees that were whizzing by "above" his head. I concentrated on flying smoothly and began a gentle climb to give him a bit more ground clearance. The Deuce was limited to 20 seconds of inverted flight, since the oil pump was uncovered when the bird was on its back. I had no idea how long he'd been out there, but it seemed like more than 20 seconds.

No one I knew in the squadron liked inverted flying well enough to try formation, especially so close to the trees. I doubted anyone had the skill to do it either. Maintaining close formation at one negative G is tough, because the controls appear to be reversed. All natural flying instincts have to be put on hold. If my anonymous wingman dropped slightly low, he'd have to push forward on the stick to come back up. If he got too close, he'd have to apply pressure toward me on his stick. It's pretty spooky—in addition to all the junk that falls into your face from the recesses in the belly of the aircraft.

I fully expected his engine to quit at any moment. We were still too low for him to eject with his head toward the ground. After what seemed like an eternity, he rolled upright, rocked his wings in salute, lit his burner and stood his bird on its tail, disappearing above and behind me.

At first, I was concerned that someone had caught me flying too low, against Air Force regulations. Then I laughed, as it dawned on me that he was far more at risk of disciplinary action than I was.

The mystery was solved when I checked the scheduling board back at the squadron. I'd been shadowed by Monty—my own flight commander. I never let him know how much he'd shaken me up. I did get even, though.

A few weeks later, a chaplain friend of mine showed me an extraordinary picture he'd taken at one of the GCI (Ground Control Intercept) sites along the Labrador coast. It showed a Deuce, inverted at about 50 feet, between two big white radar antenna "bubbles". The tail number was clearly visible. I couldn't resist the temptation

Next day, Monty and I were on 5 minute alert together. While he was pre-flighting his aircraft, I drew a crude reproduction of the photo just below his name on the scheduling board in the aircrew lounge.

"Where did you hear about that, Lehman?" he snapped as he bounded up the stairs from the hangar.

I continued to look intently at the "Outdoor Life" in my lap, and replied, "The Chaplain has a great picture of your fly-by." Chaplain Don worked for the sector commander, who couldn't ignore the violation if he learned of it.

Monty was clearly concerned. "I've got to have that picture, Chuck. Call him and see how much he wants for it."

"Sure, Monty. No sweat," I said as I walked to the phone. "Hello, Don. Remember that picture you showed me yesterday? Monty would really like to have it."

Don caught on immediately. He chuckled as he said, "Sure. Let me talk to him." Monty got on the phone, and Don asked him an exorbitant sum for the incriminating photo. Monty quickly agreed—until Don added, "But I keep the negative"

Monty was worried. Risking his buns, flying low altitude formation upside down was one thing. Risking his career with a damning photo floating around the base was something quite different. During the pause, as Monty considered his options, Don and I started to laugh.

"It's OK," Don assured him. "No one sees that picture 'till I get back to the states."

Monty smiled weakly, and mumbled, "Thanks."

Sometimes gentle revenge is sweet.

Snow and ice covered runways were a fact of life for about six months on Blue Nose bases

Blue Nose

Three of my flying assignments were located in the northern tier of air defense bases, known as the Blue Nose Zone. Ice was a fact of life for about six months a year. Usually, it was on the airfield rather than the airplanes. We flew off snow and ice-covered runways on a regular basis from November through April. There were few problems.

Several innovations minimized the risk presented by slick runways and aircraft that landed at about 160 MPH. First, the tread rubber on our main landing gear tires was impregnated with coarse steel wool. Thousands of sharp wires protruded from the tread, and gripped ice better than any automobile tire. Unfortunately, the nose wheel tires were conventional rubber—and they steered the aircraft on the ground. Second, our snow removal crews spread heated sand on the ice, whenever it got really bad. The sand stuck tight on the ice, forming a sandpaper-like texture. Third, we used a drag chute on every landing. That slotted parachute was capable of stopping the F-102 or F-106 without much braking. Finally, there was an inch-thick cable stretched across the departure end of the runway, about three inches above the concrete. We could lower a rudimentary tail hook to snatch the cable. Several hundred feet of huge ship's anchor chain, attached to the cable, would be dragged along, quickly slowing the aircraft.

Once in a while, even these measures couldn't prevent a wild ride on a 35,000-pound sled. One bitter cold January morning at Duluth, we awoke to an inch of perfectly clear, smooth ice covering the entire airfield. Weather had kept us on the ground for several days. A car was sent out to check braking action on the runway. "There is no braking action. I slid a thousand feet trying to stop from50 MPH," was the grim report. For some reason, the sanders couldn't take care of the problem. The commander and operations officer decided we needed to fly and could safely taxi to the runway if we stayed off the "snot-on-a-glass-doorknob" taxiways. We'd use the grass instead. There, the tires would crush the ice into the grass, and gain enough traction to steer.

I was tapped to lead a flight of three F-106's on a high altitude intercept mission, landing at Grand Forks, ND. They'd been spared the freezing rain. My two wingmen would fly birds just coming off alert. Our alert hangar was just off the approach end of runway 27, connected to it by a short taxiway that angled 45 degrees to the runway. They would have about 300 feet to taxi. I'd have a mile and three-quarters from the squadron area.

The ground was frozen rock-hard under the ice, so there was no tendency to sink in as I crept slowly to takeoff position. There was no way to do an engine run-up check, so I shoved the throttle forward and into afterburner, checking the gages as I accelerated. Takeoff seemed normal. My wingmen rolled 20 seconds and 40 seconds behind me. We climbed to Angels 45 (45,000 feet) and took turns being the target. We got all our assigned intercepts completed.

The fighter squadron at Grand Forks had the best Mexican food in the command. We called it El Forko Grande. We were eager to get on the ground for lunch. As we walked across the ramp, Wally asked, "Chuck, how was your takeoff roll?"

"No sweat," I replied, a bit smug at how easy it had been to fly off a skating rink.

"You mean you didn't feel that nose gear," he chided. "It was cocked 90 degrees to the left on the roll. Never did straighten out."

I felt nothing, although those tires slid sideways for about 3,000 feet. That was one slick runway—but no more so than the one at Goose Bay that got one of our jocks in trouble.

******

Ray landed just after a freezing rain and before the runway could be sanded. Several of us watched from the alert hangar as he touched down. He deployed his drag chute—but it somehow released from the aircraft and fell out onto the runway. After oscillating from side to side for a thousand feet or so, his bird suddenly swapped ends, and continued down the runway backwards!

We sat, stunned, expecting to see it lurch into the snow-banks along the runway, shear a wing and burst into flame. Instead, we saw a plume of flame from the tailpipe as he lit his afterburner. Twenty-four thousand pounds of thrust quickly stopped the aircraft. "Bet he has to change his shorts," someone offered.

******

All airplanes are pretty good kites or sails. Sometimes those aerodynamic traits can get you in trouble. One sunny winter morning, I landed at Minot, ND, after launching from Duluth. Minot had been hit by freezing rain, but the runway was OK. The taxiways and ramp were another story. As I taxied to the fighter squadron ramp, the ice became thicker and slicker. By the time I reached the parking area, there was barely enough braking action to ease to a stop. As the crewchief ducked under my wing to put chocks against the tires, a gust of wind hit my bird from the right. I sat, helpless as it slid slowly sideways, closing the gap to the next parked aircraft in line. It looked like my left wing would spear his, releasing thousands of pounds of highly volatile JP-4 jet fuel. The wind accelerated my bird. I considered trying a burst of power to move forward enough to miss the other aircraft, or at least hit his nose with my tail. I quickly realized I'd certainly hit one or more of the mobile air compressors and ground power units just ahead. That would cause a fire that would be at least as bad.

Just before impact, my left main tire hit a dry spot, jerking me to a stop. The crewchief came out from under my wing, wide-eyed, and shaking his head. "That was close!" I saw him mouth, as my engine coasted down.

******

Duluth's runway was about 800 feet above the northwest shore of Lake Superior, which is so huge that it froze over only once during the decades of the fifties and sixties. That meant easterly or northeasterly winter winds had to cross a hundred or so miles of relatively warm water before they hit the lakeshore and were lifted by the hill to runway level. Frequently, the moisture those winds had gathered from the lake surface was wrung out of them, as they climbed. The result was often incredibly heavy snow showers. They presented some interesting instrument flying challenges.

When conditions were just right, those lake-saturated winds created some of the densest fog I've ever seen. That usually stopped all flying, but one late fall evening, a couple hours after sunset, the runway was covered with a blanket of fog that was only about fifteen feet thick. I was sitting in the "Greenhouse" on the second story of the alert hangar, looking across the field toward the tower. Visibility at that meager elevation was unlimited. However, down on the runway it was about fifty feet—far less than our half-mile landing minimums.

Suddenly the console-mounted UHF radio came to life. I recognized Jim's voice. "Duluth Tower, (this is) Victor November One Six, twenty miles west, request landing instructions." He was returning from a deployment base.

A startled tower controller replied, "Victor November One Six, Runway zero niner is below minimums in fog. The field is closed. What are your intentions?"

"Roger, Duluth. My fuel gauge says I'm going to land. I can see the runway from here. How thick is that fog?"

"From the tower, the visibility is unlimited, however, ground crews say they can't see to drive. Alert Hangar, are you on this frequency?"

"I am. Jim, that stuff is like pea soup, but the top of it is just about at my feet here in the Greenhouse. I can see the tails of our birds over in the squadron area. I'd guess you've got about twelve to fifteen feet to deal with. What's your fuel?"

"I've got enough to make Minneapolis. That's about the extent of my options. They won't be very happy if I land a hot bird down there." Minneapolis-St Paul International was the hub for Northwest and a couple of minor airlines, and they didn't welcome fighters, especially with armament on board

"Yeah, you're right about MSP. Well, it's your call." I was only repeating one of the key reasons we were so thankful to be flying the hottest fighter in the world. In the fighter business, the pilot had the ultimate responsibility and authority. That was not true in some other areas of military flying, where command posts were in charge.

Jim thought a moment, then called, "Tower, I'm going to make a visual approach to runway zero niner. If it looks good, I'd like to land. If not, I'll make a missed approach, and land at Minneapolis."

"Roger, Zero Six. You're cleared to land VFR (Visual Flight Rules). Altimeter, two niner, niner five. Wind is one zero zero at two knots. We have you in sight."

At fifteen hundred feet about a mile beyond the far end of the runway, I could see the characteristic navigation lights of Jim's Delta Dart—red and green wingtip lights, a white one on the vertical stabilizer and rotating red beacons top and bottom on the fuselage. Jim flew a 360-degree overhead pattern, rolling level about half a mile out, and gliding, nose high, toward what looked like a giant lake of milk, illuminated by his landing lights.

The F-106 was designed to land about 17 degrees nose high. That put the cockpit more than twenty feet above the runway when the main gear touched down. Jim's landing lights lit up the fog as his main gear kissed the runway. I could still see his cockpit and tail. He rolled toward me at 140MPH. I knew the fun would start when he slowed to 120, and lowered his nose into the milk.

"Oh, sh...! I can't see a thing," Jim announced.

It was like driving down the freeway at over a hundred miles an hour, and not being able to see the next white dash between the lanes. For Jim, that freeway ended in a steep drop-off somewhere ahead of his nose. He had one advantage, though. The aircraft's heading indicator was very accurate. If he could hold the bird on a heading of exactly zero nine zero degrees, controlling the nosewheel steering with his feet, he'd say on the runway. Of course, the brakes on any aircraft are individual, for each landing gear, so his braking had to be precise. I held my breath as he slowed and stopped about 1800 feet from the end of the runway. About six feet of his swept tail stuck above the soup, like a shark's fin.

"I'm still on the runway," Jim called triumphantly, "but I can't see a thing. Tower, do you have me in sight?"

"Roger that, Zero Six. You appear to be in the center of the runway, right in front of the tower. You're cleared to taxi."

"I wish I could. I'll just sit here." After a few minutes he crept forward, and a bit to the right. "Tower, good news. I see a runway light."

It took about thirty minutes and most of his remaining fuel, but Jim eventually followed the white runway lights and blue taxiway lights almost two miles to the squadron ramp.

An 11th Fighter Interceptor Squadron "Deuce" over Lake Superior.

Flame Out

Ray led Victor November Blue Flight, three F-102A's. Glen on his left wing, was Blue two. I was Blue Three, on his right. We were climbing westward out of Kinchloe Air Force Base on the Michigan/Ontario border, bound for Duluth, across Lake Superior. It was a bright May afternoon and we had seen hundreds of ice floes on the lake that morning, on the way to Kinchloe. Winter had not yet released its grip.

Climbing through 10,000 feet, we could see a solid wall of clouds ahead over the lake. We tightened our formation, so that Glen and I had around 6 to 8 feet of spacing between our canopies and Ray's wing tips. That was a bit closer than standard "wing tip clearance," but we knew from experience how dense those Lake Superior weather fronts could be. We didn't want to take any chance of losing sight of Ray. He was a superb leader—smooth as silk, confident and experienced. It was easy to maintain position on him. At around 15,000 feet we entered the soup and changed radio frequency to Duluth Air Defense Sector

The controller responded to Ray's check-in call, "Roger, Victor November Blue Flight, I have you on my scope. Continue climbing at Buster (full military power without afterburner). Be advised, you have a line of severe thunderstorms 60 miles ahead of you. Tops are reported to be Angels 38." (38,000 feet)

Ray replied, "Roger, Duluth, We should be on top by that time." He glanced left and right to make sure Glen and I were tucked in tight, then focused on smooth, precise instrument flying. Our eyes were locked on him. The clouds got thicker as we climbed. At Angels 36 we were in heavy cirrus clouds, somewhere in them those thunderstorms were hidden.

"Victor November, thunderstorms are twelve o'clock (straight ahead) at ten miles."

"Roger."

It was obvious we weren't going to break out on top before we hit them. We'd have to climb faster. Afterburner power would allow us to climb much steeper. Ray checked us both again, and called, "Blue Flight, Burner …." He hesitated one second, "Now"

I saw flame leap from his tailpipe as I popped my throttle into the afterburner position. My bird slowed when the engine exhaust nozzles opened to accommodate the tremendous blast of the burner, but my burner didn't light. I was falling back fast. "Blue Three has negative burner."

I called. Just before I lost sight of him in the murk, the flame went out in Ray's tailpipe, and his nozzles closed. My throttle was already all the way to the firewall, so I moved back into position quickly.

Ray's calm voice came back, "OK, let's try it again. Burner....Now." This time I lurched forward as my burner lit, increasing my thrust by 50%—but his didn't. I was running over him. I rolled to the right, away from his wingtip, then back left to keep him in sight. Glen was having the same problems on the other side. "Lead has negative burner," Ray called disgustedly. We slipped back into position and everything settled down. Ray shook his helmet slowly and said, "All right, we'll just continue Buster climb."

"Victor November Blue, I show you entering that line of thunderstorms. Say Angels," the controller said

"Angels 36. We're still IFR." (Instrument Flight Rules, i.e. in the soup)

BLAM! BLAM! BLAM! It sounded like three fast shotgun blasts in the cockpit. My aircraft fell back so fast that I lost sight of Ray before I could call, "Three's flamed out!"

Ray's bored-sounding reply was almost comical. "Yeah. So am I."

We were flying 30,000 pound gliders. I couldn't believe it—two of us with dead engines at 36,000 feet, with thunderstorms and ice-clogged Lake Superior below us. All my flight instruments quit, so I switched to Emergency AC Power.

It didn't work! I cycled the switch half-a-dozen times with no response. "Lead, Three has negative flight instruments," I called.

"Roger, Three. I've got none either. Fire in the cockpit. Had to shut everything down." He didn't sound bored anymore. "Three, what's your altitude?'

"I'm at 31 (thousand). Airspeed is dropping below 150." I was nearing stall speed, and had no idea of the attitude of my aircraft. The only thing to do was ease the stick forward to reduce the G (gravity) load. I kept a barely perceptible pressure on the seat of my pants. The airspeed continued to drop. "My airspeed is indicating zero now," I called. I wasn't flying now. I was falling—toward hundreds of square miles of ice water.

Ray's voice crackled in my helmet, "Roger, Three. I'm indicating 350 knots, passing through 30 thousand." At least he had flying speed.

Gradually, my airspeed crept back up, as the nose must have fallen through the horizon. As it approached 220 knots, I tried to airstart the engine. No response. It had probably coasted down to an RPM too low for a start. Ray's voice came back, "Oh, oh. My airspeed is dropping fast....below a hundred."

We each went through several cycles of zero to 350 knots, keeping each other advised. Both of us were in some kind of falling-leaf maneuver, very near each other. This was getting a bit hairy. There was no thought of ejecting over all that ice water.

Again, I heard Ray. "Airspeed's coming up. What's your altitude now?"

"Twenty seven," I snapped.

I remembered something my primary flight instructor, Bobby Munch, had drummed into my head at Bainbridge Air Base, Georgia. "When your altimeter needle reverses direction, you're passing through level flight." He had stressed flying instruments with one or more of the primary flight instruments covered with cardboard. He had simulated what I was experiencing.

I was losing airspeed again. 220...210... The altimeter climbed through 26 thousand, hesitated at 26,300, and moved the other way. "Here goes nothing," I thought. Looking down at the stick, I centered it as best I could, and locked it between my knees. Maybe, if I really was passing level flight, I could hold it there momentarily. The altimeter needle didn't move.

"Level Flight," I thought!

I still had no idea if I was right side up, inverted, or somewhere between. Only one instrument in the cockpit was powered by DC. The turn needle had been useless during the gyrations and thunderstorm turbulence. Now I noticed it was nearly centered. Maybe I was "wings level."

I tried another airstart. No luck.

Ray called, 'Three, I've got this thing running. How you doin'?"

"Another No Joy (failure). What's your altitude now?" I replied.

"Twenty one. I'm heading 260 for Home Plate (Duluth).

"What about your fire," I asked.

"Guess the smoke in the cockpit had something to do with the flameout. I'm OK."

At least one of us was going home.

"One more try," I thought. This time the engine fired up just like it did on the ground. The AC power came back on line, the gyros wound up—and I had flight instruments again. They were all screwed up, but they were working. The attitude indicator showed 35 degrees left bank, but it had to be wrong because the turn needle showed no turn. The aircraft was level. No sweat.

Actually, my winter flight suit, bunny boots and parka were soaked with sweat. As I turned toward Home Plate, I thought of the guys in pilot training who hated instrument flying, and detested "flying" the Link, a primitive box-like, ground-born instrument trainer. Bobby Munch had even irritated me with his insistence on flying the "gauges" with most of them covered. "Thanks, Bobby," I said aloud.

I called Ray, "Blue Lead, this is three. I've got a good airstart. Altitude is 12 thousand. I'm turning to 180 (south) to get away from the lake. Where are you?"

I could hear the smile in Ray's voice as he said, "Roger, Three. Good on ya! I'm at 10 thousand, heading 260, and I'm VFR " (in the clear)

I dropped the nose and popped out of the clouds over the coldest looking lake I've ever seen. We didn't bother to join up.

I entered visual traffic at Duluth and landed. As soon as my rollout airspeed permitted, I opened the canopy. Cool, sweet air rushed in. Thousands of birch trees were beginning to bud. Their aroma was wonderful.

What a great welcome home!!

C-47 "Gooney Bird"

Gooney Bird

Sometimes flying can be downright ridiculous—like the first time I flew the famed Gooney Bird. The ubiquitous DC-3 (civilian version) or C-47 Gooney Bird was put into service in 1933 and has been so successful that it's still around. Great, great, great grandchildren of the original pilots could be flying them today. In 1960, the Goon was closer to the 1903 Wright Flyer than to the sophisticated F-106 that I'd been flying.

In the spring of that year, I came down with a bad case of boat fever. One day the squadron commander heard me talking and said, "Chuck, I've got a great boat for sale. You should take a look at it."

I was interested. He explained that he'd left the fifteen foot Chris Craft in Michigan when he moved to Duluth. His description made it sound like the perfect boat for our family. The kids were too young to water ski, so we'd use it mainly to cruise some of Minnesota's 14,000 lakes.

"There's a Gooney Bird going over to Selfridge Air Force Base this afternoon," he said. "Why don't you ride over and take a look at it. You can come back with them tonight."

I called Marian, then walked down the ramp to Base Operations. The pilot of the old C-47 was more than happy to take me along.

I settled into one of the red web-sling "seats" that hung from the uninsulated aluminum walls in the cargo area. As he poured the coal to the two old Pratt and Whitney radial engines, I wished I'd brought my helmet. The noise was deafening. The old bird lifted off and its landing gear came up one by one. This strange behavior earned its nickname. Real gooney birds are tropical sea birds who raise their webbed feet one at a time after a running takeoff. We'd been airborne about fifteen minutes, when the pilot came back, and yelled into my ear, "Will you take the left (aircraft commander's) seat for a while. I don't feel so good." He didn't *look* so good.

I strapped into his vacant chair, and greeted the copilot. He was a young guy about twenty-four, named Dick. An array of vintage instruments graced a well-worn panel. I noticed four gauges, plus the magnetic compass that were supposed to indicate aircraft heading. No two of them agreed. "How do we get these heading indicators slaved to magnetic?" I asked. He looked at me like I was some kind of a nut.

"Beats me. They were like that when we took off."

I returned the look in kind. "What Flight Service Station are we supposed to be talking to?"

"Shoot, I don't know. The major was handling the radios."

Same look.

"OK," I said, half-heartedly. I asked several other basic questions without getting any useful information. Finally, I frowned at Dick and asked, "How much time do you have in the Goon?"

"I've never been in one. I'm a helicopter pilot." He paused, "How about you?"

"I rode in one once," I replied. "I'm a 106 jock. I don't know anything about trash-haulers." Anything with more than one engine and room to carry something was a trash hauler to a fighter pilot. One of my pilot training instructors had told me that any airplane big enough to go to the bathroom in was too big to fly. He didn't say it quite so politely. I liked the advice, though.

"Well, so be it," I thought. "I'm aircraft commander of a three decades-old trash hauler, with a copilot who knows less than I do." As I picked up the ancient hand microphone, I considered calling in as "White Cane Flight." The blind was indeed leading the blind.

"Flight service, this is Air Force 34189, level seven thousand. Request radio check." That seemed like an innocent way to find out whom we were supposed to be talking to.

"Air Force 34189, this is Marquette Radio. We read you five-by" (loud and clear) came the immediate reply.

"Ah ha. That's more like it," I thought. "At least we're back in touch with the world and I didn't have to reveal my ignorance." That was highly important to any fighter jock. I fumbled to get one of the primitive navigational radios tuned to Menomonee, on the shore of Lake Michigan. We never did get the heading instruments slaved to the reliable, but imprecise magnetic "Whiskey Compass." We could get by with it despite its several inherent errors. There was really no need for any instruments, other than the altimeter and airspeed. The weather was beautiful and I knew that part of the world like the back of my hand from several hundred hours of looking down at it from the F-106. Finding Selfridge was not a problem.

As we started across Lake Michigan, I checked the engine instruments. All the pointers rested in the green-shaded part of the dials. Both big Pratt and Whitneys purred loudly about ten feet behind the cockpit. Airspeed was 100 knots, less than one sixth of the cruising speed of the 106, and well below the speed where the Six would have fallen out of the air.

I thought of the Gooney Birds that had flown millions of tons of war materials and troops during World War II.

They had even towed wooden gliders into combat. Some had dropped paratroopers onto the hottest areas of the big war. A few had even landed behind German lines to rescue pilots or to insert special teams. Most impressive to me was the fact that Gooney Birds had flown "The Hump" over the mighty Himalayas to supply China's fight against the Japanese. This did not feel like an airplane I'd like to fly through four mile-high mountain passes.

For probably half an hour, I forgot poor Dick in the right seat. I was used to the tight confines of a fighter cockpit, doing everything myself and making all the decisions. I hadn't even let him touch the control yoke. It was a massive partial steering wheel mounted on a column that was hinged at the floor. The thing had a heavy, truck-like feel, quite unlike the feather-light touch of the stick in the 106. There was no hydraulic boost on the Gooney Bird's controls. The big yoke was functional in that it let the pilot use both hands to muscle the aircraft around when necessary.

Dick and I finally took turns flying the Goon, navigating by pilotage (looking at the ground). We ran into a headwind over Michigan. It subtracted from our 100-knot airspeed, giving us a groundspeed of around 70. For the most part that kept us ahead of most of the cars and trucks on the highway. A few went past us and disappeared over the horizon. I thought of the 106, clicking off a mile every 2.3

seconds at top speed. Still, it was a beautiful day to just poop along with plenty of time to think, rather than reacting in milliseconds to the little tasks and problems of flying.

After a couple hours of less than exciting droning, I saw Detroit ahead, changed radio channels and called, "Selfridge Tower, this is Air force 34189, fifteen miles northeast. Request landing instructions."

"Roger, Air Force 189, you'll be landing runway 35. Wind is 010 at seven knots. Altimeter, 30.19. Call turning base." (crosswind leg of the traffic pattern)

I remembered enough from primary pilot training to know that piston engines liked a rich fuel mixture and high RPM during descent. As we left 7,000 feet, I pushed the mixture and propeller RPM levers all the way forward. The big engines roared at a higher pitch. It seemed we probably should lower the wing flaps part way, but neither of us could figure out how to do it. "Oh well, " I yelled at Dick, "If we pull the throttles back, we should go down." It was only partly in jest.

We leveled off at traffic pattern altitude, downwind, parallel to the runway and about a mile to the side. "Selfridge, Air force 189 is on downwind."

"Roger 189. I have you in sight. You have no other traffic. Check gear down."

I glanced across at Dick. He was looking intently at me. "Dick, put the gear down," I said. He gave me that look again. He searched his side of the cockpit, then stared across at mine. "How do I do that?" he pleaded.

"Just put the dad-gummed handle down!" I realized helicopters didn't have retractable gear, and felt bad for the tone of my voice.

"What handle?"

I reached forward to the left side of my instrument panel, where gear handles are supposed to be. Nothing remotely like the typical handle with a little wheel and tire on the end was anywhere in sight. There was about 30 seconds of searching on both sides of the cockpit. We turned up nothing. We found three strange levers that looked like they might have something to do with hydraulics. Most landing gear are moved with hydraulic pressure. Dick tried each of them in turn. The hydraulic system groaned and whined—but nothing moved. The wheels were tucked up tight in the engine nacelles.

"Tower, Air force 189 is turning base."

"Roger, 189. Check your gear."

"I wish he'd quit saying that," I said to Dick. Then to the tower, "Ah, Selfridge, ah, stand by."

We ran through the drill with the handles again with no better results. It was time to turn toward the runway, onto final approach.

"Tower, 189 is turning final."

"Roger, 189. Check gear down."

"Ah, tower, 189 will make a low pass down the runway, gear up. We'll go out and re-enter traffic," I said humbly.

We flew the approach down to 200 feet. I added power to maintain that altitude, and we cruised down the runway. Not exactly the high-speed passes I was used to. At the far end of the runway, I shoved the throttles forward. The roar of full power must have roused the real aircraft commander. He tapped me on the shoulder and asked, "Do you want me to land this thing?"

Dick looked at me. I looked at him. We both laughed. I turned to the major. He looked sleepy, but a lot better. "Either land it or put the blasted gear down," I said.

He slipped into my seat, worked some magic with those same three handles, and the big fat tires tumbled out of their wells. They locked down. The Major greased that old goon onto the asphalt with a gentle squeak.

I still don't know how to put the landing gear down on a Gooney Bird.

The T-28 Trojan

Flying Blind

Sometimes human physiology can cause unexpected and severe problems, even in aircraft with modest performance. I learned that lesson the hard way, early in my flying career.

The T-28 Trojan was a homely, not quite ugly, stilt-legged, two place trainer with a 700 horsepower, seven cylinder radial engine that turned a ten foot long, wide blade propeller. As the second aircraft in our training, it was quite a step up from the little T-34. The big beast felt as brawny as it looked.

One afternoon, I was scheduled to fly a solo cross-country mission from Bainbridge, Georgia to Dothan, Alabama, and return. Puffy, white cumulus clouds dotted clear blue skies along the route. At breakfast that morning, I'd noticed a slight stuffiness in my head. It was not even enough to be called a cold. I had simply cleared my ears a few times, using the valsalva maneuver (holding my nose, and blowing with my mouth closed to "pop" my ears) then forgot about it.

The mission went well. It was easy to pick out checkpoints along the route. Towns, bridges, railroads and water towers matched their respective symbols on the map that was clipped to my right leg. The winds at my altitude of 7,000 feet were light enough to be insignificant. I arrived back in the Bainbridge training area on time and happy with a very easy sortie.

I called the tower for landing instructions and began an en-route descent. Almost immediately, I felt pressure behind both cheekbones—the on-set of a sinus block. We'd had enough aviation physiology to recognize what happens when the passages into the sinuses get plugged and refuse to let air flow back into them to equalize the increasing atmospheric pressure during a descent or a dive. Bad things start to happen.

By the time I reached 5,700 feet, the feeling of pressure in my maxillary sinuses had graduated to intense pain. The frontal sinuses behind my eyebrows joined in. I used the valsalva until my ears threatened to blow out, but no air entered my sinuses. There was no choice, but to level off and try to decide whether I could land the aircraft.

The Trojan still had 30 minutes of fuel remaining, so there was no immediate danger. I climbed a few hundred feet and, predictably, the pain decreased. When I resumed the descent, the pain returned. After several of these cycles and watching my fuel gauge move toward empty, I decided to try to bust through the pain level, hoping the increasing pressure would eventually overcome the blockage.

A few hundred feet lower, the pain became a four alarm, eye-popping maelstrom. Then I went blind!

It started with darkness in my peripheral vision and quickly progressed to total darkness. The pain was unbearable. I eased back on the stick, and jammed the throttle to the firewall. As the bird began to climb, the lights came back on. However, every time I resumed my letdown, my vision would be cut off. The fuel gauge continued to drop. Clearly, I was not going to land the bird.

Again, I climbed. This time, I tightened all my parachute straps and reviewed the bailout procedures in my mind. The tower responded to my emergency call, asking what they could do to help.

"I'm eight miles northwest of the base. Every time I try to get below 5,000 feet, I lose my vision. I've got ten minutes of fuel remaining. If this sinus block doesn't clear before then, I'll be bailing out. Have someone pick me up".

I knew I'd be blind during the parachute descent, but at least there was a good chance I'd get down OK and get medical attention.

"One more try," I thought, as I climbed back to an altitude where I could see. I hesitated there, saying a quick but sincere prayer. Starting down again, the pain came back with a vengeance. My sight began to go, too. Somewhere inside my head, I heard a squealing, gurgling sound. The pain stabilized. My vision stayed clear. With five minutes of fuel remaining, my sinuses were slowly filling with air.

I landed with enough fuel to taxi to the ramp. The flight surgeon was waiting. I deserved the lecture I got.

Never, ever fly with a cold—or even the puny beginnings of one.

The sharp nose, wedge shaped windscreen and 60 degree Delta wings of the "Deuce" and the "Six" were not prone to icing...most of the time.

Ice

It was a typical winter night at "The Goose", as we all called Goose Air Base, Labrador. There was a low overcast with intermittent snow showers. The ceiling averaged 300 feet. Visibility varied from ten miles between showers to one half a mile in them.

I'd run some intercepts against a T-33 target aircraft at medium altitude, about 150 miles north of the base. At Angels 28 (28,000 feet) it was a magnificent night. There was no moon to compete with millions of stars, brilliant as they can be only far from civilization. Curtains of green and red Aurora Borealis danced in the northern sky. It was great to be alive and a privilege to fly a fine bird.

My F-102A Delta Dagger was performing flawlessly. We affectionately called it the Deuce. All four of my intercepts had resulted in easy M.A.'s (mission accomplished). My wingman had equally good luck on the first three, but had radar problems on the last. I heard the disgust in his voice as he called our ground control site, "Joe Penner, this is Hotel Lima Zero Eight, M.I. (missed intercept). Request pigeons to home plate." He wanted direction and distance to The Goose, so he could check his TACAN navigation system.

The controller answered, “Zero Eight, your pigeons are 175 degrees at 165 nautical miles.”

“I cut in. “Zero Eight, this is Zero Six. I’ll join up on you and we’ll RTB (return to base) together.”

“Negative, Zero Six. I saw you break north after your last intercept. I broke south. You’d chase me half way home trying to join up. Besides, I’m bingo fuel.” He needed to get back to Goose, so he’d have enough fuel to divert in case the weather went sour.

“Roger that. See you on the ground. I’ve still got 4500 pounds.” I saw his red rotating beacon among the stars, miles to the south. The target had already headed home. I decided to enjoy the solitude and beauty of the night. Forty-five hundred pounds of JP-4 were more than enough to loiter for half an hour, get home and still have enough to reach Harmon Air Base in Newfoundland. Diverting to Harmon seemed unlikely. Throughout the mission we’d gotten regular weather updates. Those snow showers only occasionally lowered the visibility to landing minimums.

I turned south along the Labrador coast, obscured by the undercast six miles below. Even on that heading I could see the aurora. It was one of those nights when I just didn't want to land. Finally, after thirty minutes, I called Joe Penner and told them I was letting down toward The Goose. I switched radio channels. "Goose Approach, this is Hotel Lima Zero Six about 30 miles east, passing twenty one thousand. Request a GCA (Ground Controlled Approach)"

"Roger, Zero Six. I have contact. You'll be landing Runway 27 at Goose. Ceiling 200 feet, visibility one half mile in snow showers, wind 290 at 18 knots with snow and ice on the runway," they replied.

"Hmm, field minimums," I thought, "Eighteen knots and no blowing snow?" Not great conditions, but by Goose standards, not bad. I'd get some good instrument practice.

"Zero Six, turn starboard to 265, descend to 2500 feet."

At that altitude I skimmed less than 100 feet above the clouds. They were flat as a skating rink.

"Zero Six, you're twelve miles out. You have a KC-135 at twelve o'clock (straight ahead) five miles. Descend to 1500. Weather is now 300 feet and one mile."

"That's more like it," I thought. At 1500 feet, my navigation lights and red rotating beacon illuminated the clouds. I was inside a pulsating pink cocoon. Red instrument lights reflected off the canopy, distorted by its curvature. Even after five years of flying all-weather fighter interceptors, the magic of hurtling through that cocoon at several hundred knots fascinated me. I lowered the landing gear and flipped the landing lights on. Huge snowflakes came at me like rifle bullets. "Whoa. They're not kidding about those showers," I thought. No sweat, though. The weather was still above minimums and I had enough fuel to reach Harmon if it went bad. GCA did a great job of directing me down the three-degree glide slope, right on centerline. At about 250 feet I still hadn't broken out. "Only 50 feet to go to minimums," I thought, "But if I don't see the approach lights, I can press a bit lower."

An excited voice crackled in my helmet. "Zero Six, go around! Go around! The aircraft ahead of you has not cleared the runway."

"Roger. Zero Six on the go," I snapped, thinking, "What in the heck is that guy doing on the runway. He was five miles ahead of me". I shoved the throttle to full military power and raised the gear handle. As the Deuce "cleaned up" it accelerated quickly in the cold air.

The GCA controller came back on the horn and said, "Sorry, Zero Six. That KC had some kind of problem on the runway. He's clear now. I'll give you a closed pattern. Maintain runway heading and climb to 1500."

"Roger. Zero Six is already level 1500," I answered. A few seconds later he turned me south for about a mile and a half, then east to parallel the runway.

"Check gear down, Zero Six. We'll keep this one in close," he instructed.

At 220 knots, I lowered the gear—and immediately felt the aircraft buffet. It felt like a stall warning, but I was nearly 90 knots above stall speed. I pushed the throttle forward and turned the landing lights on. It was pouring rain. In the glare of my landing lights it looked like a hard summer shower, not the sort of rain you might expect on a winter night. The runway temperature was about 25 degrees, so I figured it would be around 20 at my altitude. The aircraft was also cold-soaked from two hours at minus 60 degrees at altitude. My jet was an ice-magnet. Still, I couldn't believe the problem was ice. The Duece just did not ice up very often. It's sharp 60-degree swept wings, needle nose and sharply raked windscreen shed ice very well.

As my airspeed crept toward 240 knots the buffeting stopped. "Approach, it looks like Zero Six is in some pretty severe icing conditions out here. Keep me in really close".

"Roger. I copy," he answered. The tone of his voice betrayed that he didn't understand what ice could do.

Final approach and the glide slope were at least three minutes away. Then, it would take another two and half or three minutes to reach the threshold of runway 27. The buffeting returned. Airspeed was still 240 knots—maximum with the gear extended. I kept adding power. Still the Deuce shuddered like it was about to fall out of the air. Finally the throttle bumped against the military stop. Full throttle and still buffeting! Not good.

"Approach. Zero Six is icing up. You've gotta get me on final, quick," I said with a bit too much bite in my voice.

"Do you wish to declare an emergency, Zero Six?" he asked.

"Negative," I answered, then thought of Marian and the kids, snug in our base house only four miles away, and added, "Correction. I am declaring an emergency."

"Roger. Turn port to 310," came the reply. He was angling me onto final approach to save time. It was a very gentle turn, but it caused the buffeting to increase. I was riding a stall at military power. Using the afterburner was out of the question, except as a last ditch effort. It would provide plenty of power, but in the Deuce, the exhaust nozzles opened before the burner lit. That meant an abrupt loss of thrust just before the burner ignited. If the burner failed to light, or hesitated, I was bound for half-frozen Lake Melville.

"Unless you can start me down the glide slope soon, I may have to leave this thing," I said. The thought of ejecting over the lake was almost as distasteful as riding the bird into the water.

The controller responded to the situation and advised, "Come port to 290. Begin your descent now."

"Roger. That will help," I replied. I let the nose drop a bit in the turn. The buffeting stopped for just a moment. Gradually, it came back. Even in a thousand feet per minute rate of descent and an airspeed of 75 knots above normal, with the throttle against the wall the Duece was riding a stall. I glanced up from the instruments. Still raining.

"Approach, you'd better alert rescue. I must have a huge load of ice," I called.

"Roger, Zero Six. I've already called them." He was rising to the challenge.

This was going to have to be the best precision approach I'd ever flown. If I settled below the glide-slope, I'd never get back up. On the lakeshore, between me and runway threshold, was a big tank farm filled with millions of gallons of volatile jet fuel. "Oh, well," I thought, "If this rain doesn't let up, that's academic. I'll never get that far." The only thing to do was nail the approach. The Deuce was a stable instrument flying platform—but not tonight. Sweat ran down inside my oxygen mask as I struggled to keep the sluggish beast on the glide-slope.

At 600 feet, I looked up again at the glow of my landing lights. SNOW! Never before or since has snow looked so good. I was finally out of the rain.

"Zero Six, you're on glide-slope, on centerline, one mile from touchdown. Emergency vehicles are in place."

"Thanks. I may need the barrier," I answered. At the far end of runway 27 was a one-inch thick cable, stretched three inches above asphalt. By lowering a hook on the belly of the Deuce I could snag it and begin to drag several hundred feet of ship's anchor chain. As more and more chain was snatched from both sides of the runway, it would stop the jet. Since I'd be landing at least 100 knots too fast on snow and ice that seemed the probable outcome.

The bird was still shuddering when I finally saw the approach lights. There would be no chance to flare for a smooth landing and the Deuce was never known for particularly strong landing gear.

As my landing lights picked up the stark white runway, I raised the nose a few degrees—and quit flying. The aircraft slammed onto the runway like a Navy fighter hits a carrier. The gear held.

I yanked the drag-chute handle just as the gear crunched into the snow. A satisfying tug announced a good chute. Still, the little fir trees that lined the runway to give some depth perception for daytime landings in whiteout conditions, flashed by at an alarming rate. The chute and 18 knot headwind soon slowed the Deuce to taxi speed, so I called the tower, cancelled the emergency, and taxied to the 59th Fighter Interceptor Squadron ramp.

The crewchief chocked the wheels, and came out from under the left wing shaking his head in disbelief. He pointed to the aircraft as dozens of other maintenance people came running for a look. The main landing gear had about a foot of clear ice on their leading edges. The wings had nearly eight inches. I stood next to that ice-covered Deuce, mentally thanking the engineers who came up with those incredibly efficient delta wings, the controller who modified my approach just enough—and the One who's hand was on the stick with mine.

Marian had a wonderful dinner on the table when I walked in.

"How was your flight?" she asked.

"Routine. Just routine."

Welcome to "The Goose"

Greetings

There were times when flying at "The Goose" was almost too much fun to be real. We were privileged to be able to do things that would have resulted in disciplinary action anywhere else. That was partly due to the remoteness of Labrador and partly to the personalities of our commanders. Since no roads marred our corner of Canada, there were no witnesses to "unusual" flying away from the field. On base, only our wonderful Canadian hosts could see what we did. They never complained.

The Goose Air Defense Sector (GADS) commander was a WW II fighter pilot, son of a Hollywood producer, with a flair for the flamboyant. He loved to taunt non-fighter pilots, especially the Strategic Air Command (SAC) guys who came from US Bases to Goose to pull their alert a little closer to their Soviet targets.

Late one summer evening, Minor and I were on 5-minute alert when the red phone rang. Usually, that happened only after the klaxon horn announced a scramble. I jumped up from my "Outdoor Life", and dashed into the glassed-in cubical that served as our communications center.

"Alert hangar. Captain Lehman speaking."

"Chuck, this is Colonel Milner. I've got a good one for ya. Who's out there with you?"

"Captain Nelson, sir. What can we do for you?"

"There's a SAC two-star (Major General) inbound in a C-118. I want to give him a real Goose Air Defense Sector (GADS) welcome. His ETA (Estimated Time of Arrival) is 2047 (8:47 PM). I'd like you and Minor to scramble at 2030. Go out over Lake Melville and orbit. I'll have the tower keep you informed about his landing and taxiing on the field. Now, this is going to require perfect timing."

This was sounding good. He continued, "When they roll the stairway up to his bird in front of the terminal, I want you two in formation, on the deck, coming up behind him at 400 knots. Ideally, when he steps onto the platform, I want one of you on each side of the tail of that 118, with your burners just lighting. That should get his attention."

"Yes, sir!" I exclaimed. This was a fighter pilot's dream; a legalized buzz job, in show formation, for an unsuspecting "audience." However, this one was at night. It was low! Finally, if we arrived straddling the tail of that transport a few seconds too early or too late, the impact would be lost. "Thanks for the opportunity, Colonel."

"I know you can pull this off. Oh, by the way, I'm part of the greeting party, so I'll be at the foot of those stairs," he concluded.

"This better be good," I thought. Minor and I discussed the mission. I was so pleased to have him flying my wing. He was one of the best "sticks" (pilots) in the 59th FIS, smooth, confident and unflappable. I'd flown his wing many times, and had always been impressed with his talent. I felt honored to be leading this one. No matter what we had to do to make this work, Minor would be glued to my wing. That made it a lot easier.

We took off in formation and flew out over the lake. No moon illuminated the inky black. Only the lights on the base and a few meager bulbs in the little village of Northwest River, about 30 miles northeast, gave any evidence of a horizon. Lake Melville was about 150 feet below the airfield elevation. We intended to use that difference to hide our approach from anyone but the guys in the tower. We'd pop up over the bank to start our run down the ramp. If everything went well, the general would have no warning.

"Hotel Lima Zero One Flight, your C-118 is ten miles out. He'll be landing on Runway 27 in about six minutes. I'll give you a call every mile of his approach," the tower called.

"Thanks, Goose. We're orbiting at 500 feet, seven miles east," I responded.

We watched the C-118 fly over us on his final approach. I wondered if the general was looking down and wondering what our navigation lights represented.

"Hotel Lima Zero One, your C-118 has just touched down."

"Thanks, Goose. We're standing by."

Goose Tower gave us a play by play of his taxiing to the far end of our mile-long ramp to his parking spot in front of the passenger terminal. The controller sounded as excited as we were.

"Zero One, the 118 is in the chocks. They're rolling the steps into position. You're cleared for a high speed pass."

It was music to a fighter pilot's ears

I remembered the last time Goose Tower had cleared me for one of these. Actually they requested it. They had visitors in the tower. I made the run as close to the tower as was safe. When I pulled up, the guy in the tower said, "Can you give us another one and make it a little higher. They'd like to see the side of the F-102, now." I thought the top should have looked pretty good.

It was time. "Zero Two, let's push it up," I called to Minor. We eased our throttles forward, and accelerated to 400 knots, as we turned toward the Goose. Skimming over the black water at 100 feet, I glanced to the left at Minor. He was tucked in tight, his red instrument lights illuminating his face.

"Hotel Lima Zero One, they're opening the door of the 118."

"Roger, Goose. We're two miles out," I replied.

We popped over the shoreline bank, into the thousands of white, blue and red lights that illuminated the field. I hadn't expected the confusion those lights would cause. From traffic pattern altitude they formed a familiar array that outlined every facility on base. Streaking along at about 50 feet, they were a meaningless glare.

The radio call to light our afterburners was supposed to be, "Zero One Flight, burner," followed in one second by, "Now." My problem was estimating the time to the 118's parking spot, hidden somewhere in that maze of lights. I couldn't pinpoint our own position, either. Finally, I saw one of our squadron buildings flash by.

"Zero One Flight, burner....," I called—then realized it was the wrong building. "Ready ....," I stalled for time. The 118's rotating red beacon appeared in my windscreen, dead ahead at 200 yards. "Now!"

My burner lit just as the 118's tail flashed by my left wingtip. Minor had moved out just enough. He was just beyond it. Our two thirty foot burner flames reflected off the vehicles surrounding our guest. The sound must have been more than deafening.

"Yeah Hoo!" I yelled into my oxygen mask, as I pulled up into a closed traffic pattern. Minor took spacing in the turn and we landed.

"Zero Two. This is Zero One. Sorry about that burner call. I was disoriented," I called sheepishly.

I thought I heard a chuckle in his voice as he answered, "No sweat, Zero One."

We walked up the stairs from our parking bays in the alert hangar. The red phone was ringing. It was Colonel Milner.

"That was incredible. Your burners lit just as he stepped onto the platform. Hell of a noise!! He almost jumped off. You guys done good!"

Sometimes you just get lucky.

The F-86L was barely supersonic.

Mach One Plus

For more than four decades, the question most asked when people learned that I flew fighters is, "What does it feel like to go supersonic?" I'm sure the answer is disappointing. The short answer is, "It feels pretty much like flying subsonic, only things happen a bit faster".

A classic example is the magnificent F-106 Delta Dart, which I'm told still holds the world speed record for single engine aircraft—1526 MPH. It was smooth and quiet at that airspeed, as it was at any speed. However, it was fascinating to watch the miles tick off on the TACAN (Tactical Air Navigation) indicator. A mile went by every 2.35 seconds. Suppose you fly for one hour at that speed. Since you are relaxed and at ease, your eyes blink once every two seconds. Each blink lasts 1/50 second. In that hour you'll travel more then eleven miles with your eyes shut. You need to think ahead and plan ahead at that speed.

A longer answer to the perennial question about supersonic flight, is that it depends a lot on the design of the aircraft you're flying. For example, there was a dramatic contrast between flying beyond the Mach (Mach one is the speed of sound at sea level) in the F-106A and the TF-102. The 106 was so sophisticated, and so aerodynamically clean that it was literally in its element above Mach one. The two seat (side by side) trainer version of the 102 had a frontal area about like a greyhound bus. Pushing it through MACH one was an unforgettable experience. It shuddered and made noises that tried to convince you not to keep the throttle to the firewall. One of these beasts that I flew at Duluth was waiting for me years later when we moved to Goose Bay. Aircraft 54040 had a real personality and treated pilots to an interesting ride. The bird was so badly warped that its huge, three-panel canopy would not seat against the rails. Even with the rubber seal fully inflated, there was enough space under the left front corner to stick your index finger out into the slip-steam.

Once, when another Deuce was joining up, I yanked a stack of papers off my kneeboard, and shoved them under old "Forty- Forty's" canopy. The pages exploded into confetti along the fuselage, definitely getting the attention of the pilot trying to impress us with a perfect join-up. I won't quote his comment.

My first experience with the Mach was in an F-86L in 1958. The L was an improved version of the Korean era Saber Jet. It carried twenty-four 2.75-inch diameter rockets in a retractable pod under the cockpit.

We learned to intercept "enemy bombers" on a 90-degree beam attack. Picture yourself approaching a street intersection at 600 MPH. On the crossing street is another vehicle at about the same speed. You adjust your speed so he will cross the intersection a hundred feet ahead of you. Just before he crosses, your fire control system shows the fire signal. You squeeze the trigger and two dozen rockets form a shotgun-like pattern ahead of you, catching him broadside. You pass just behind him, or what's left of him. At night, this was quite exciting. In the weather, where you could only see him as a blip on a radarscope, it was downright spooky.

The L was barely supersonic. To get it through the Mach, you had to light the afterburner, and accelerate to the transonic range (.95 to .99 Mach) then "bunt" the nose down a little, so gravity could assist the J-47 jet engine. In the transonic range, the L's nose got heavy and needed a bit of nose-up trim for level flight. Without trimming, the nose dropped on its own. The only indication of going through the Mach was a momentary jump in all the pressure instruments, i.e. altimeter, airspeed and vertical speed. The Mach meter would settle down above 1.00.

That nose tuck was a real problem for the early would-be Mach busters. Several pilots were killed by what was then interpreted as control reversal. Finally, Captain Chuck

Yeager, in the Bell X-1 rocket powered experimental aircraft, got through the Mach and lived to tell about it.

I had the very great privilege of working for him years later, when he was a Brigadier General and the Director of the Aerospace Safety at Norton AFB, CA. One evening he invited me to go with him on a speaking engagement in Redlands, California. I was delighted. I'd read of his exploits, but had never heard him tell his story.

We were in a classroom, packed with admiring people. As General Yeager humbly and simply described that first supersonic flight, they were riveted on him in obvious awe. One tiny old lady in the front row leaned forward to take in every word. She was in her eighties, but obviously sharp as a tack.

The general finished his story and asked for questions. There were several. He answered them all with humor and grace. The old lady was so excited, she was shaking. She raised a tiny, thin hand, and asked, "General, that's so exciting. What did it feel like to go faster than sound?"

General Yeager's eyes sparkled as he walked over to her and bent down slightly. "It was pretty good," he said, "but not as good as sex." The room exploded and she looked at the floor, her cheeks glowing crimson. After a few seconds, she threw her head back and joined the laughter. Chuck Yeager has the most delightful, unassuming personality of any true hero I've known.

That was pointed out again a few years ago, when Marian and I stopped in Grass Valley, California to see him. At first, the old Yeager sparkle seemed dimmed. He had only recently lost his beloved Glennis and was obviously hurting

Hoping to get the conversation on a more pleasant note, I asked, "General, are you still flying?" He was about seventy at the time. His eyes lit up. "You bet," he said. "I go down to Edwards once a month, and fly the F-15 and F-16." Then that great Yeager grin spread across his face, as he continued, "You know, every time I go down there, those young studs polish their swords." He knew every fighter pilot alive would like to defeat the legendary Chuck Yeager in an aerial fight. "But no one has beat me yet." To me, that epitomizes the spirit of a fighter pilot.

He knew those young jocks were the cream of the Air Force crop. They had the 20/10 eyes, the lightning reflexes and the burn to win—but he had a half-century in the cockpit of a fighter. I read a few years later, that Chuck Yeager had flown his last mission in an Air Force fighter.

I'm betting he's still undefeated.

Mane Event

One of the grand old traditions among fighter pilots was capturing squadron mascots. Most of these icons were inanimate, but they ranged from moth-eaten works of taxidermy to a cage full of very live Canadian lynx. Elaborate battle plans were concocted to "liberate" them from their rightful owners. Some of the mascots made the rounds, across the country and around the world, being stolen by one squadron after another. These escapades fostered esprit-de-corps, and kept alive the intense competitiveness that sets fighter pilots apart.

In the spring of 1962, I became an unknowing accessory to one of these capers. Four of us were returning to Duluth from a formation cross-country around the southwestern U.S. We decided to RON (remain over night) at Schilling Air Force Base in Kansas. It had been a long day, with several aircraft problems along the way, so I had dinner at the club and went to my room to bed. I assumed the other guys did the same.

Next morning we all showed up at Base Operations to plan and brief our final hop. Gary was leading. Win was number two. I was three. Bob was number four. We cranked up and checked in by radio with Gary. Bob failed to check in. We saw him shut down and climb down the ladder, helmet in hand. He was aborting. My exotic MA-1 System, which controlled nearly everything on the 106, failed to come on line, so I was forced to do the same. We'd briefed that if anyone had a broken bird; the rest of our flight would press on home. The aircraft were needed there for five-minute alert and training missions.

Bob and I walked across the ramp toward Base Ops. A very upset Aerodrome Officer met us at the door. "Where are those other two 106's"? he demanded.

"They got off about five minutes ago," I said, wondering how anyone could miss the ear-splitting blast of two F-106 afterburners.

"Damn!"

"What's wrong"? Bob asked.

"Which one of you has our lion's head"? He demanded, getting even redder.

"Lion's head? What lion's head"? I asked, trying not to laugh. I thought Gary and Win had been a bit too eager to get airborne without us. The major fumed and sputtered, as he told us someone had removed their prized male lion's head from the wall behind the stag bar at their officers' club. Club employees had discovered the theft about 10:30 PM and had alerted the security police. Dozens of cops searched the base for hours, but for some reason, none of them thought of the four F-106 pilots in the BOQ (Bachelor Officers' Quarters)

Schilling was a bomber base, so it was easy to understand their paranoia at losing something so tempting. A fighter outfit would have quickly developed a plan to retake the lion—or grab something else from the offending squadron.

We were grilled for half an hour, but it was easy to avoid giving the major any information. We had none.

By late afternoon our birds were repaired, so Bob and I flew home. We got the "skinny" on the lion's head as soon as we found Win. He and Gary had hung around the club until about 10:00. They'd noticed the lion was alone in the stag bar. They merely stepped behind the bar, where Gary stood on Win's shoulders, removed the head, wrapped it in a checkered tablecloth and slipped out the back door.

As they started for the flight line, police cars seemed to come from everywhere. Search-lights scanned every dark corner. They dove into a drainage ditch and lay there in the muddy water considering their options. One of course, was to discard the head and walk back to the BOQ. That would have been admitting defeat—and their mud-soaked orange flight suits would have been a slight giveaway.

They noticed the ditch angled toward the flight line where our birds were parked. Since they were already wet, it seemed logical to stay in the ditch, below the searchlights and crawl to the edge of the concrete and hope there was some way through the fence. They did, and there was. The ditch turned into a culvert at the flight line. The fence was just loose enough that with both of them lifting, they could just squeeze the head under it.

Somehow, no one saw them crawl under their aircraft. They opened the armament bay doors on Gary's bird. There was no rope and no time to tie the head to one of the missile rails, so Win lay on his back and balanced the trophy on his up-turned boots. The armament bay doors on the 106 were closed by compressed air at 3,000 pounds per square inch. When the switch was moved to "close" they slammed shut in the blink of an eye. Yet, somehow the head ended up on the inside and Win's boots on the outside. It must have been those fighter pilot's reflexes that helped him get his feet out of the way in the nick of time. There's no logical explanation.

The mangy head made quite a trophy. We ceremoniously installed it at our fighter club the next Friday night. Someone noticed a small, tarnished brass plaque on the back. It said simply, "Museum of Natural History, London".

Gary laughed, and slapped Win on the back. "Those bomber pukes actually stole this thing in England. I didn't think they had the balls."

Maybe it's just a pilot thing.

Chuck (far right) with Instructor, Bobby Munch (center) and "Table Mates" Charlie Brown, Gerald Petty and Bob Buckles.

Double Immelman

Lightly made decisions can be costly in flying—especially when you have very little experience to help you overcome a poor one. Such was my first attempt to do a Double Immelman.

The North American T-28 Trojan was a giant step up from the T-34 Mentor, the first aircraft we flew in primary pilot training at Bainbridge Air Base, Georgia. The Trojan's 700 horsepower radial engine cranked out more than five times the power of the Mentor. It's cockpit and canopy were huge for a single engine aircraft. The bird sat very high off the ground on long landing gear to provide clearance for a twelve-foot long, two bladed prop. When the two trainers were parked side by side, the David and Goliath comparison was inescapable.

From the initial ride, I loved the ugly T-28. Imagine quintupling the power of your car! The Trojan felt big, tough and mean.

We got one ride in the traffic pattern, making normal landings, and one doing basic maneuvers and emergency landings. The instructor in the back seat would suddenly jerk the throttle to idle and call, "Forced landing." We'd pick out a farmer's field, attempt to glide to it, lower the gear and flaps and fly to within 50 feet of the ground. The instructor would push the throttle back up, so we could climb back to altitude—and do it again. Once the instructor was convinced we could put the bird into a field safely in case the engine quit, we'd get a solo ride or two. Then we moved on to aerobatics.

Rolls, Loops, Cuban Eights, Spins, Lazy Eights, Chandelles, Immelmans and Clover Leafs were learned in turn. The Immelman turn was probably the most practical. It was developed by a German WW-I pilot as a way to reverse direction in a vertical plain. He probably faked out a lot of allied pilots when he started turning vertically instead of horizontally.

The Immelman was simple. You merely apply full power, lower the nose to pick up the desired airspeed, then pull back on the stick to bring the nose up and over in a half loop. At the top, you roll from inverted flight back to normal flight—and you're going back the way you came, but at a higher altitude, Usually, the pull-up requires about four G's (four times the force of gravity).

I'd overheard a couple of instructors talking about a double Immelman. It sounded easy enough. At the top of a normal Immelman, you simply use what airspeed you have left after the first vertical climb, to do another one. That puts you on the same heading as when you began the maneuver. They didn't mention what type aircraft they were talking about, but I assumed they meant the T-28. Big mistake. I didn't hear anything about entry airspeed, or what speed you should be looking for at the top of the first Immelman. Details.

A few rides later, Bobby Munch turned me loose to practice aerobatics solo. I could hardly wait.

I flew a couple of each of the required maneuvers, including the Immelman. All went pretty well. My confidence soared. It was a beautiful South Georgia day. Puffy white cumulus clouds dotted a deep blue sky. I climbed above them and flew to the north edge of our aerobatic training area.

A pair of clearing turns convinced me I was alone. I shoved the throttle to the firewall and pushed over into a 20-degree dive. The T-28 rumbled and vibrated as the airspeed needle approached the red line, indicating maximum safe speed. I let the needle nudge the line, then pulled back smoothly to around six G's. That was the max I could handle. My vision grayed, as centrifugal force drained blood from my head. I tightened my leg and gut muscles to stem the flow into my legs, and concentrated on keeping the wings level. At the top, I eased off on the backpressure and watched color come back into the sky and the ground over my head.

I rolled quickly upright. At that point, I should have checked to see how much airspeed remained. I probably did—but since I had no idea of what it should be, I simply started pulling up again. Long before I reached six G's the aircraft started buffeting, indicating an approaching high-speed stall. I held what G force I could without stalling the wings. Just after passing the straight up attitude, the controls got mushy.

Before I could react, my control stick lost all resistance. It felt disconnected. It was. My airspeed had fallen to zero. With no air flowing over the control surfaces, the stick did nothing. When the T-28 stalled, it normally went into a fairly gentle spin. I knew how to recover from a spin. I yanked the throttle to idle and pushed the right rudder pedal to the stop, trying to force a spin. That did nothing. The aircraft refused to spin.

By now, green fields, blue sky and white clouds were swapping positions with astonishing speed. The tail section made weird sheet metal noises as the Trojan fell backwards, tumbling and rolling.

Altitude, 5,100 feet. Dropping fast. I checked my parachute straps, feeling more concerned about being washed out for stupidity than for my own hide. With my aircraft gyrating like it was, I doubted I could get out, anyway. I was running out of altitude and ideas.

There's a mythical pilots' malady called a Fecal Syndrome. Sometimes in a really tight spot, a small piece of feces dislodges from the large intestine and gets into the blood stream. When the fragment passes through the brain, it's impossible not to say, "Oh, sh…!" I did.

Finally, in desperation, I slammed the throttle all the way past the sea-level stop, put there to keep pilots from blowing up an engine by over-pressuring it. That seemed a minor risk. The tremendous torque delivered by the engine to that huge prop really made the aircraft wind up. Gradually, though. The airspeed needle crept off the peg.

The oscillations decreased. The nose fell below the horizon—and I was flying again! There was just enough altitude to recover from the resulting dive without scaring the crap out of two unsuspecting cotton farmers on green tractors.

Lesson: To avoid Fecal Syndromes, consider the possible consequences of all flying decisions.

Bobby Munch was waiting when I walked, sweat-soaked into our briefing room. "How'd it go?" he asked.

"I learned a lot."

When there were no missiles on the rails,
they could carry some strange things.

Seafood Express

Flying can be a really messy experience. For several years I was a staff officer, doing Tactical Evaluations and Operational Readiness Inspections of flying units. That made me a true "Headquarters Weenie" in the eyes of most fighter pilots. I got my flying time with several different squadrons, although my favorite was the 11th FIS at Duluth, because it was familiar and I liked the scenic country along the north shore of Lake Superior.

Providing flying time for headquarters people was not high on the priority list for most squadron commanders, who were usually strapped to get enough time for their own pilots. Despite that, the commander and all his troops always made me feel welcome—until one fall evening in 1968.

I flew into Duluth in a T-33 trainer, parked it at base operations and walked a few hundred yards to the 11th FIS parking area. Lt. Col. K was just climbing down the ladder from an F-106. His smile was genuine. "Hi, Chuck. How's everything at the Head Shed?"

"Just great, Sir. Any chance of getting a night sortie tonight?" I asked hopefully.

"As a matter of fact, I've been saving one for you. How'd you like to fly out and back to Tyndall?"

"You bet!" I replied. "This cold wind off the lake makes Florida sound pretty good, even for a short stay. I can sure use the night time."

"OK, here's the skinny. We're having a big party tomorrow night for the whole base. I want to surprise them with something special. It's oyster season down there, so I called a buddy to pick up four sacks of fresh ones. I'll have the CAC (Combat Alert Center) call him when you're airborne and he'll meet you at Base Ops to help you load 'em. You should be back here by 2200 (10:00 PM)"

We often hauled stuff on the missile launch rails inside the armament bay of the 106. I'd never tied seafood onto those rails, but I was eager to get some night flying and the 3,000-mile round trip to the Florida panhandle sounded better than a single local sortie. "That's fine with me, Colonel. I can be off in an hour. Thanks."

"Glad to help, Chuck. Oh, just let the CAC know your ETA (Estimated Time of Arrival) back here and I'll have someone unload those sacks and put them in the club's walk-in fridge," he promised.

I filed an instrument flight plan at Flight Level 450 (45,000 feet). There was never any traffic up that high, so I'd have no delays. By 1700, I was climbing in afterburner. The 106 was built to climb, so it could intercept enemy high altitude bombers, even if they got close without being detected. I checked in with Minneapolis Center. The controller replied, "Roger, Victor November Zero Nine, report level at 450."

I couldn't help smiling, as I quickly called, "Roger, Minneapolis, Zero Nine is level at 450."

I knew what his next transmission would be. "Zero Nine, what is your type aircraft?" he asked, disbelieving that I could be that high only a little over two minutes after take-off.

"Zero Nine is an F-106A."

"Oh!," he answered. Controllers had a tough time comprehending a 70,000 feet per minute initial rate of climb, when airliners were climbing at one-tenth that rate. As usual, it was peaceful and solitary at Flight Level 450. I set my speed at .95 Mach (95% of the speed of sound) Somewhere over Illinois a near-full moon burst over the eastern horizon, lighting my cockpit and the geometric farmland below. It was a perfect night to fly—the kind that magnifies the magic-carpet quality of single seat, high performance flying.

Even the ubiquitous Florida coast thunderstorms had bowed to the evening cool. Only puffs of white lined the northern edge of the Gulf. I landed at Tyndall feeling great. No one met me at the fuel pits, but I assumed Col. K's friend would be at Base Ops with four bags of fresh oysters. He wasn't.

Nobody there had heard anything about him or the oysters. I waited. Gradually, my mood changed from moonlight bright to thunderstorm dark. After an hour, I bummed some change from the coffee kitty, replacing it with a dollar bill and went to the pay phone. There were several oyster companies nearby. On the third call, I spoke to a "Good-Old-Boy" who remembered an order for "some Air Force guy from up north."

"Hallelujah." I exclaimed. "Those are the ones. Can you bring them out to Tyndall?"

"Nope. I'm here alone. Y'all will have to fetch 'em yourself…and pay for 'em."

Lightning flashed from my thunderstorm mood. "Great," I said. "Where are you? How far from Tyndall?"

"Jist down the road a piece, on the Gulf Coast Highway."

"How big a piece?" I growled.

"Oh, 'bout twenty miles, I'd say. I'll be here another half an hour. Then I'm lock'n up. Y'all better hurry, ya hear?"

"Yeah, I'll be there." I hoped there was a cab on base. The dispatcher called the local taxi company for me and five minutes later a ramshckle, vintage Ford rattled up the drive. I jumped in. "Bubba's Oyster Shack." I said.

"Where the heck is that?"

I imitated the guy on the phone, "Down the Coast Highway a piece."

"OH."

He turned out of Tyndall's main gate, toward Mexico Beach. I wondered how he knew down the road was that direction. I hoped the Good-Old-Boy had said down, not up. Twenty minutes later we squealed to a stop, followed by a blue cloud of exhaust smoke. A rotund man with four inches of cleavage above the back of his filthy jeans was just snapping a rusty padlock on a door that looked like it could be broken into with a nail clipper.

"Y'all the guy for the oysters?" he asked. At his feet were four bulging burlap gunnysacks, resting in a widening puddle of slimy seawater.

"That's me," I said with obvious disgust. "What do I owe you?"

He smiled through two broken teeth. "I made a mistake. The boss left a note. They're paid fer. Y'all can just take 'em."

"Things are looking up. Thanks." I reached down to pick up a sack, and a horrified voice behind me wailed, "Not in my cab, you don't. You ain't putting them things in Esmeralda, y'hear."

I walked toward the multi-toned yellow heap he was so fond of. "Yes we are—if you want to get paid. There's some black plastic over there behind that old boat. That should keep Esmeralda's trunk clean." I was more worried about contaminating the oysters than soaking his car.

He reluctantly released the thick rope that held the trunk lid. It squeaked open and sure enough the inside was covered with a motley collection of greasy tools, oil cans, fishing gear and beer cans almost covering an oil soaked carpet. "Just lay that plastic in there and help me load these."

Our stomachs and thighs were soaked with aromatic oyster juice as we rattled toward Tyndall. He was silent. Well, almost. I just couldn't understand what he was muttering. At Base Ops, I paid him and unloaded the sacks while he watched.

I had filed a round-robin flight plan, so I carried the bags, one by one to my aircraft, while a lone maintenance troop watched in disbelief. "You gonna put those stinking things in that beautiful airplane?" he asked.

"I am and I'm going to need some rope. Can you hustle up enough to tie these to the four missile rails?"

He was off in a flash—a bit too eager to be away. He came back with a big coil of quarter inch rope and a jackknife. By then, I'd realized what his boss would say if he came into the hangar with his freshly starched fatigues soaked in oyster juice. I was already wet from belly button down.

"I'll open the armament bay. Then, I'll try to balance one of these on my shoulder and hunch it up to the rail. You just tie it on." By the time we'd done that four times, I was soaked from the ears, down. He was laughing. I closed the bay doors and he helped me strap in, being very careful not to touch my flight suit.

High clouds had moved across the Midwest, so there was no scenery on the way home. The moon painted the cloud-tops stark white. Oysters tainted the cockpit air. I was glad to be breathing 100% oxygen. At Duluth, I let down through 35,000 feet of clouds into lake-effect rain, and landed about midnight. I was eager to turn my cargo over to Col. K's representative.

There was no one to meet me.

I asked the crew chief if he'd seen anyone waiting.

"No, Sir. This flight line is dead. I haven't seen anyone since the local birds landed two hours ago."

I was wet, stinking and seething. There was no one at the squadron, either, except for a single airman in the CAC. I told him that his commander's cargo was in the armament bay of aircraft 082, said good night and walked to Base Ops.

Thirty minutes later, I was airborne in my T-33. The sun was not quite up when I landed at Colorado Springs. On my drive home it began to light the Front Range of the Rockies. That gorgeous sunrise revived my mood. I was a bit concerned about what I was doing to the seats of my prized '56 Ford, but I laughed about the F-106, sitting on the ramp at Duluth, dripping smelly liquid onto the 11th FIS ramp. I vowed I wouldn't go back.

My beautiful wife was in bed when I slipped into our bedroom. She looked up, sniffed, wrinkled her nose and said, "Uff, where on earth have you been?"

Dropping my ripe orange flying suit as I stepped through the shower door, I said, "That's a long story, Honey."

****

Actually, my experience as a seafood delivery pilot was mild compared to the poor Navy, F-4, Phantom jock I met at Naval Air Station New Orleans a year or so later. As I taxied to the ramp in my F-106, I noticed him, leaning against one of the drop tanks on his aircraft. I parked and walked by him on the way to the operations building. He looked so forlorn, that I asked him what was wrong. "You won't believe it," he said, without looking up.

"You look like you just had your back-seater eject on final approach. What did happen?" I asked.

"How could anyone be so stupid?" he said, almost under his breath.

"Who? You?" I asked, reaching out to shake his hand.

"Yeah, me—but not only me. Notice anything different about this drop tank?'

I looked behind him, and noticed a small door had been installed in the top of the tank. It was latched tightly with cam-lock fasteners. "Looks like someone who's really good with sheet metal, converted that tank into a giant baggage pod."

"They did, indeed—and that beautiful pod has twelve hundred dollars worth of fresh seafood in it," he replied.

It was about 90 degrees on the ramp, so I said, "I suppose your bird is broke and the stuff is spoiling while you wait for someone to fix it."

"There's plenty of crushed ice in there with it. The bird is fine. I spent the whole squadron party fund on seafood for our skipper's farewell bash."

"That should be a great party. So, what's the problem?"

"There's several hundred gallons of jet fuel in there with the goodies! What am I gonna tell the boss?" He was almost in tears.

The transient maintenance troops had refueled his bird without noticing the neat door in what they thought was still a fuel tank. I was no help with his dilemma, but it sure put my little fiasco into perspective.

Wildlife

Woodland caribou are fascinating creatures. Their whitish "Santa's Reindeer" appearance and group mentality make them easy to spot from the air. Large herds migrate across Labrador each year, searching for tender lichens and moss. During the winter of '63 I'd watched about a hundred of them from altitude for several days, waiting for a chance to check them out up close.

One sunny afternoon, I finished my assigned training with enough fuel to go hunting. The caribou were feeding on top of a bald, round-topped mountain about thirty miles southeast of The Goose. A fair sized river flowed from its base into Lake Melville. I decided to surprise the animals at close range, rather than just fly over them. The Deuce had enough power to climb the steep side of the mountain on the treetops.

I let down over the Lake and flew up the river toward the foot of the mountain, thinking I was alone. However, that day another hunter was flying. Ray had also been keeping track of that herd. He, too, had some extra fuel. On the back side of the mountain was a long canyon angling to the southeast—almost exactly the opposite direction from the river. Ray was in that canyon.

I cruised up the river at treetop level to the base of the mountain, then pushed the throttle to full military power and started up the slope. It appeared I'd arrive at the bald spot at about 375 knots. As the final trees flashed beneath my wings, the slope shallowed out to the rounded top I'd seen from altitude. I eased the stick forward to follow the contour. By the time I reached the caribou, I was close to a zero G (no apparent gravity) condition, due to my curved trajectory. Caribou scattered in every direction. They hadn't heard me coming.

WHUMP! My aircraft lurched, as gray and red flashed over my canopy—close. Very close! I was sure my vertical stabilizer was gone. I pulled up hard; hoping to get some parachute-opening altitude before my bird came unglued. The jet responded normally. I knew Ray was in the air, but had no idea we were anywhere near each other.

"Ray, was that you"? I squeaked.

"Yeah!" came the equally high-pitched reply.

For a few seconds we thought we'd hit each other at nearly 750 knots closing speed.

On the ground, we checked the aircraft for damage. Neither had a scratch. We both had felt the impact—kind of like meeting an eighteen wheeler on the highway at 800 MPH. Ray shook his head. "Good thing they didn't put one more coat of paint on these birds, or we be in a million pieces on top of that mountain." It was that close.

Sometimes God protects those too dumb to protect themselves.

******

The lure of wildlife affected my flying again some years later in Colorado. I was flying a T-33 jet trainer at the time, while assigned to the Air Defense Command (ADC) Headquarters in Colorado Springs. On a bright September afternoon, Jim and I were scheduled to make a staff assistance visit to one of our units in Montana. Aspens in the mountains along the way were dripping gold. It was a magnificent day. Jim was at least as much of an outdoorsman as I was, so we decided to stay at low altitude and enjoy the spectacular Colorado scenery.

Low altitude mountain flying in a light aircraft is very dangerous, due to violent downdrafts generated by high winds blowing across the ridges and forming oscillating waves. Low performance aircraft don't have the power to climb out of these "Mountain Wave" downdrafts and often get slammed into the rocks. In a jet, these concerns are minimal—as long as you keep your airspeed up. With enough speed and the power that's available, it's not much of a problem to zoom out of the strongest drafts. So we could relax and enjoy the ride.

We flew across the South Park Plateau, finding two herds of beautiful brown, black and white pronghorns. They flashed their white rump patches in alarm, and scattered as we passed over them. A few elk fed peacefully in one high meadow near the Wyoming border. As the dense fir forests gave way to sagebrush canyons in Wyoming, we noticed a pair of coyotes hunting rabbits. They were at the mouth of a broad canyon, rimmed by rocky ridges, about two thousand feet high.

I circled once, descending, and we entered the remote canyon on the deck. The place was a coyote heaven. As we skimmed the sage dozens of the little dogs scurried out of our path. Jim was excited.

"Look at those buggers go. It sure would be fun to come up here with a rifle and a varmint call."

"Yeah," I replied, "but it would be a heck of a walk. We haven't crossed a road in thirty miles."

"Just my luck. We find a perfect place where the ranchers might appreciate a little help, and we can't get in. Maybe with a horse," he added hopefully.

"Not me. It would be fun, but I'm not riding any horse that far." It didn't seem like a place for a casual ride.

The canyon began to narrow, and we were soon enclosed by rocks 50 yards off each wingtip. Ahead a steep, brush covered slope closed the canyon's northern end. I glanced at the airspeed; 315 knots—plenty to zoom over the ridge, even without adding power. I planned to clear the rim by 50 feet, or so.

As I pulled up, a big coyote scrambled through the rocks on our left. When I looked forward again, the windscreen seemed filled with a guy on a big brown horse. He was right on the edge of the canyon—and we were headed straight for him!

"Oh, s…", I yelled, as I snatched the throttle to idle and pulled up sharply. I hoped reducing the engine noise and getting some vertical separation would avoid spooking the horse. My pull-up was pretty brisk—about 5 G's. Jim had no warning to get ready. The force drained enough blood from his head to black him out, momentarily.

"What the hell was that all about", he sputtered, as his vision came back.

"Some guy on a horse. We darn near hit him." I pushed the throttle back to climb power and racked the bird into an 80-degree left bank, looking back over my shoulder. The canyon rim was deserted. We circled once. Nothing. The rider had vanished. There was a dense clump of trees near where I'd last seen him. I hoped he was in it and still in the saddle.

"You know, some cowboy is going to have a great story to tell around the campfire tonight".

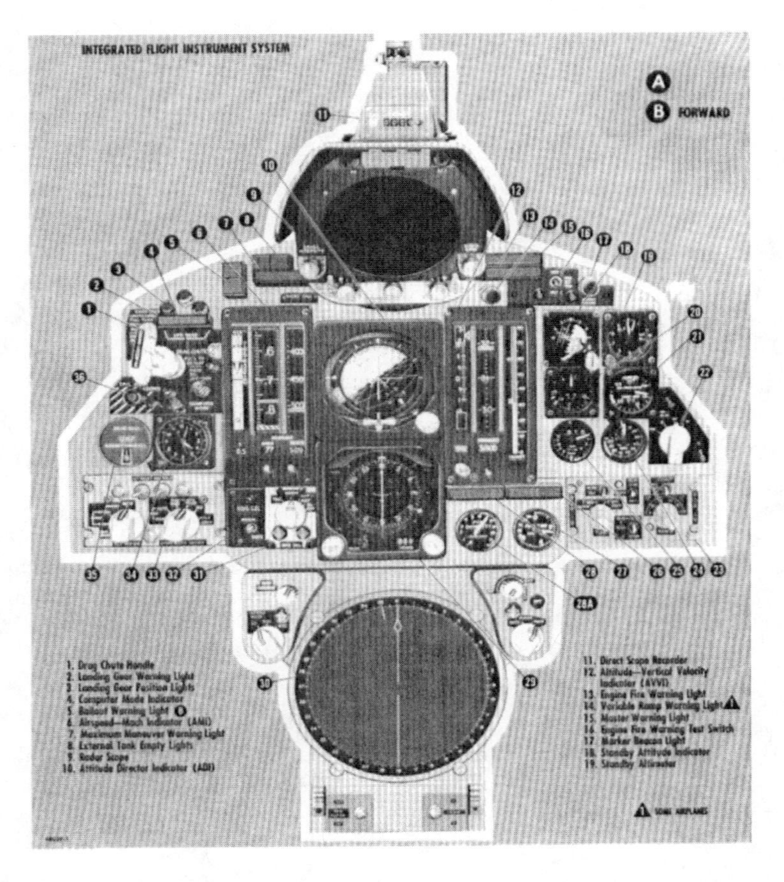

The vertical moving tape instruments in the F-106 made instrument flying easier than round dials.

D.C. Descent

Don was the son of a lobster fisherman. Maine had colored his personality with the patient persistence of that ilk. His dream was to own a lobster boat and support his family just as his father had done. Until that time, flying the F-106 was a pleasant diversion. He was a good flight commander who set high standards. He also blessed the eight of us in the flight with the time and opportunity to learn.

One stormy night over our Nation's Capital, my training got pretty intense.

Our flight had been given two Six's for a weekend cross-country. Don and I were most eligible for a "Navigational Training Mission", so he suggested we go to Dow Air Force Base, Maine, near his home. His folks would treat us to a real Down East lobster boil. I was easily convinced.

He explained that we'd get some formation work in during the first leg, from Duluth to Andrews Air Force Base, outside Washington, D.C. Half of that leg and the approach into Andrews would be at night. Weather at Andrews wasn't expected to be too great, so we'd probably be in the soup. Night weather formation in the Six was never much fun, but it was vastly superior to the Deuce, because the Six's navigation lights were arranged to give a wingman some indication of the lead aircraft's attitude. That helped a lot. Still, when Don said he'd like to fly my wing, I didn't argue. Maybe I should have.

We got off the ground an hour before sunset. Duluth SAGE controlled us to the edge of their coverage, then passed us off to Madison. We bored through the dark from one SAGE Sector to the next, with Don maintaining loose formation. It was a peaceful, moonless night, and I could almost taste the feast that awaited us in Maine. Unless we somehow lost our primary SAGE control, we wouldn't even need our TACAN (Tactical Air Navigation) System.

Don's red rotating beacon flashed through my cockpit every second or so, momentarily lighting up my instrument panel. Red-lit flight instruments and engine gages stared back, reflecting their distorted images from my curved canopy glass.

The Six had a revolutionary Integrated Flight Instrument System. Instead of a cluster of round instruments, it had a series of printed tapes, which rotated past a stationary horizontal lubber line to read out altitude, airspeed, angle of attack, vertical speed and Mach number. Above the lubber line was a round Attitude Direction Indicator (ADI) that showed eight items related to aircraft attitude. Below the line, a Horizontal Situation Indicator (HSI) displayed eight more items related to navigation. Between our legs, a Tactical Situation Display (TSD) about the size of a dinner plate, showed a tiny F-106 that moved across a projected map of the ground. It provided heading, ground track, range for the fuel remaining, the position of any flying target and the optimum heading to attack that target. The system provided a huge amount of information that was easy to read. It greatly simplified instrument flying. However, the key word was "Integrated". It was all tied into the MA-1 System—and it's vacuum-tube-driven digital computer was prone to fail. When that happened, most of the great information went with it. Also, in early 106's, we could only tune nine TACAN Stations. Normally, that was no problem. F-106 units usually operated over a few hundred miles of U.S. and Canadian air space, where nine channels were enough.

Don and I had asked maintenance to program Andrews and several enroute TACANS into our MA-1's. We assumed they had done so.

Somewhere over West Virginia we entered cirrus clouds. I concentrated on flying smooth instruments. Don was tucked in tight. I could feel his bow wave pushing gently on my left wing. We were handed over to Washington Approach Control, and things started to go downhill. We flew into an area of severe thunderstorms. Lightning flashes lit Don's aircraft, and semi-blinded us for several seconds at a time. Instead of offering to vector us to the final approach at Andrews, where we could have picked up the Instrument Landing System, they cleared us to fly a jet penetration off Baltimore TACAN—which was not in our computer. At the same time, they directed us to a radio frequency that our computers didn't have. We had to work the radio problem first.

There was a way to tune the communication radio manually in the cockpit, but it would be very difficult for Don. Four tiny rollers on the console next to our left hips set the frequency. I could look down in the dim red light at the miniscule numbers on the rollers, and change them one by one. Don would have to move away from me slightly, change one roller, look back at me, check and correct his position, then repeat the drill for each roller. At night in the soup, it was downright dangerous. I protested to Washington Approach. That did no good. They were having ground radar problems. Don got it done—without falling off my wing. We resumed radio contact with Washington Approach.

However, without the TACAN navigation system, there was no way to fly the penetration (descent). A maintenance guy once showed me that by removing the TACAN control box from the right console and prying off it's rear cover, you could see a rotor with little pips that depressed micro switches to change frequencies. By pulling up on them with a fingernail, you could reposition them and bypass the computer. When everything was put back together, the TACAN would be on a new station. Doing it at night, while flying in weather, was a bit like repairing your watch by the glow of a Christmas tree bulb, while driving down the freeway at 70MPH with another car in the adjacent lane—steering with your knees.

I explained what I was going to attempt. He had heard of it and agreed.

There was a small screwdriver in the left sleeve pocket of my flight jacket. It would remove the four screw-lock fasteners that held the control box in the console. I looked out at Don. I could only imagine what he was thinking. With the control stick clamped between my orange-clad knees, I went to work.

Two screws loose. Thirty-degree left bank. "Damn!" I rolled level. Two more screws. A thousand feet per minute rate of descent. Gently, I eased back up to Flight Level 410 (41,000 feet) I apologized to Don. By the time

I got the back off and the pips repositioned, I'd put Don through several more gyrations.

Finally, I slipped the box back into its hole. Baltimore TACAN popped up on the HSI. I looked at Don. He was still hanging on, shaking his head slowly.

The approach was a piece of cake.

As Don and I walked across a puddle covered ramp, toward Base Operations, we decided to RON (remain over night) at Andrews, and head for Maine in the morning.

"What a ride," he muttered. "Tomorrow, I lead."

Baggage pod is just behind the main landing gear on this F-33

Photo courtesy of Pat's World F106DeltaDart.com

Watermelons and Trash

Minor Nelson and I hit it off from my first day in the 59th Fighter Interceptor Squadron. He was a tall, lanky, slow-talking Texan. Despite the minimal animation in his speech, he was sharp as a tack and a really good "stick". No one in the outfit handled the F-102 "Deuce" or T-33 "T-Bird" any better. Best of all, Minor was the most unflappable pilot I've ever known. No one understood "Cool" in those days, but he was.

We were assigned to the same flight, one of four in the squadron, each with about nine pilots. I felt privileged when the scheduling officer paired us up. In our off time, we hunted and fished together.

When Minor learned his brother was getting married in Texas, he requested, and got a T-Bird for a weekend cross-country. These navigational training sorties, as they were known officially, were designed to keep us sharp in flying the civil aviation route structure. On local training missions, we were controlled by Ground Control Intercept Officers.

Minor asked me to go with him to Webb Air Force Base in west Texas, a round trip of about 5,000 miles. In the T-Bird, that was six hops (legs, in airline terminology).

The three hops to Webb were uneventful. The wedding went well. Saturday evening, Minor suggested we take home a surprise for our families. The necessities of life were usually available at The Goose, but many luxuries were not. That included perishables such as watermelons. It was melon harvest time in West Texas.

The T-Bird had no cargo or luggage space at all. Our wedding clothes had traveled outside the bird, in a small pod, slung beneath the fuselage. It was neither heated nor pressurized. At the T-Bird's normal cruising altitude of above thirty thousand feet, the temperature is about 60 degrees below zero, year 'round. However, we felt that if we could stow our clothes inside the T-Bird's tiny cockpit, and if we could jam the melons into the pod, we might be able to fly home at low altitude without freezing them solid.

Minor and I walked into the local super market, dressed in our blaze-orange flight suits, polished black boots and black baseball caps adorned with the black bat of the 59th FIS. There was a huge pyramid of watermelons near the cash registers. We began to inspect them—but we didn't look much like shoppers. Within minutes, the manager was standing behind us.

"May I help you"? He asked with obvious suspicion.

Minor matched his Texas drawl. "Yes, sir. We're looking for two watermelons to take up to Labrador."

"Labra… what? Where is that?"

"It's 500 miles north of Maine," I responded

"I didn't think there was anything that far north, 'cept maybe Eskimos. Who'd want to eat watermelons in that cold?"

It's pretty hot up there, now," Minor said. "The eighteen feet of snow we got last winter is almost gone."

The manager's jaw dropped. "Eighteen feet! They close the roads here when we get three inches. Why are you so fussy about what you buy? Those melons are all good."

"I'm sure they are, but we're taking them back there in a jet trainer," I said.

"Oh." The manager mumbled, and walked away.

Two minutes later he was back. "Look, you guys have handled at least twenty-five melons. What's the problem?"

I grinned, beginning to enjoy his frustration. "Like I said, we're taking them up there by jet. Say, have you got a yardstick we could use?"

"Yeah, I guess so."

While he went for one, Minor and I exchanged knowing looks. The manager had no idea what we were trying to do. We thanked him for the yardstick. Minor took melons off the stack, and I measured their diameter, while the poor manager shook his head in dismay. "Why do you have to measure my watermelons? You said you were flying them to the Far North."

"We are," I said, "But they're not riding in the airplane with us."

"Oh." He disappeared, talking to himself.

Moments later, he was back. By now melons surrounded the disassembled pyramid for two yards all around. We explained the baggage pod, and finally found two long, narrow melons, close to the maximum ten inches in diameter. To his obvious relief, we re-stacked the pyramid before paying for the melons.

When we got to our bird, and crawled under it, we found we'd mis-measured just a bit. They were too big! While Minor held the melons at the mouth of the baggage pod, I flopped on my back, and stuffed them in with my feet. The melons were a press fit.

We stayed below 18,000 feet on the trip back to The Goose. The extra fuel consumption at that altitude required one extra hop—but we got 'em home—frozen solid. No one complained. Fresh watermelon is a treat, in the Sub-Arctic, even when it's been frozen.

******

As fighter pilots, we made fun of those who flew big

airplanes. They were lumped into two categories: Bombers and Trash Haulers. That mock disdain may have been a bit misplaced, at least for the Trash Haulers. We did a bit of strange carrying of goods ourselves.

For example, when I got my assignment to Goose Bay Labrador, I asked my commander at Duluth if I could take a T-33 up there to check the place out. I was eager to see The Goose—but I had an ulterior motive. I had just gotten a nice Minnesota whitetail deer and a Wyoming antelope. I sure didn't want that fine meat to go to waste. A friend who had preceded me to The Goose agreed to store the meat in his freezer if I could get it to him. The T-33, T Bird, was too cramped to carry much of anything. Two small "Fighter Bags" could be crammed into a tiny pod slung under the belly. However, the T-Bird was an offshoot of the F-80 Korean era fighter, so it had a gun and ammunition bay in the nose. Most of that bay had been filled with communication and navigation gear, but there was room between the black boxes to stuff small packages—like frozen meat. I managed to squeeze about 200 pounds in there and still force the doors shut.

On takeoff, the nose seemed a bit heavy, and we needed more than normal airspeed to get the nose wheel "unstuck," but the bird flew OK—that is, until we got on final approach at Goose. Long before we got slowed to final approach speed, I ran out of trim, and was putting a lot of back-pressure on the stick to keep the nose up. Finally, I couldn't hold it, even with both hands, and asked Joe, in the back to give me a hand. He was the only really spooky pilot in the whole squadron and that really shook him up. He did get on the stick in the back seat, though, and between the two of us we planted the bird on the snow-covered runway without busting the gear. Better yet, he never told anyone.

I was pleased to know my meat would be waiting when I got up to Goose permanently. I thought I'd done something unusual, until I got to know some of the guys in my new outfit, the 59th Fighter Interceptor Squadron.

One described how he'd brought his tropical fish to the Goose in the tight cockpit of the F-102 Deuce. The fish rode in a large plastic bag on his lap. He had even modified an air pump to operate on 24 volt aircraft power, so the little guys wouldn't get hypoxic (oxygen deprived). Another pilot carried his bicycle, strapped to one of the missile launch rails whenever he went cross-country. We learned that lobsters, which we could buy for 50 cents apiece in Newfoundland where we had a detachment of two fighters on alert, could be brought back to Goose in the upper electronics compartment of the Deuce without freezing or dying from lack of oxygen. Hundreds of fish from the unspoiled steams and lakes in Newfoundland traveled the same way.

My own ultimate trash hauling exploit involved about 500 pounds of moose, caribou and bear meat, a couple dozen live lobsters, plus a bunch of trout and salmon. I was bringing one of the alert Deuces back to The Goose for periodic maintenance, just after a very successful hunting and fishing trip on Lake King George the Fourth. One of the under-wing drop tanks on my bird had been removed and replaced by an eight-foot-long chaff dispenser. It was empty, so I decided to get all the meat home in one load. The missile rails were all draped in bags and boxes, the upper electronics bay was packed with packages of frozen meat, as was the chaff dispenser.

It was a beautiful, moonlit night, so I thoroughly enjoyed the flight across the Straits of Belle Isle. At one point I remember thinking, "Gosh, if I prang this airplane, and the accident investigators find five or six hundred pounds of 'remains,' they're going to be really confused as to who or what was flying it." Morbid? Yeah, I guess so, but not that unusual. Accidents were a lot more common then, and we all had good friends "Buy the farm."

When I pulled into the chocks at Goose, someone rushed out to open the chaff dispenser. He almost fainted when he saw all that meat. We did a lot of entertaining with that meat.

Sometimes it's worth it to be a trash hauler.

Deuce over Lake Melville, Labrador

Photo Op

Minor and Robby Dale Nelson were due to leave The Goose about a month before Marian and me. We had all enjoyed the special beauty of Labrador and had lots of pictures, but we had no good ones of the Deuce in flight. Minor and I wanted some shots of the F-102 with some of Labrador's spectacular landscapes in the background.

We finally got scheduled to fly together on a low-level mission, and agreed to bring our new 35mm cameras. After our normal mission briefing, we discussed the pictures we hoped to get. We would take turns being the "model" and the photo-ship, flying over the Mealy Mountains, Long Lake, Muskrat Falls and magnificent Labrador Falls. At each place the one taking the pictures would position his aircraft to get the best angle. The "model" would fly loose formation between the photo-ship and the natural wonder. It sounded simple. Of course, all this was before the advent of point-and-shoot cameras, so it took two hands, to set aperture, shutter speed, focus, frame the shot and take the picture. At 300 knots, that had to be done quickly—while flying the jet with your knees. Flying without hands is no precision drill, but it's doable.

With Minor on my wing, I knew that I had to merely get us into the right position and avoid running into something. He would be between me and the target. He seemed to trust me, too.

We completed our training mission, joined up, and flew southeast to the snow-capped Mealy Mountains. We each got our pictures. Long Lake and Muskrat Falls went equally well. We each got what we hoped would be memorable shots.

No sweat—or so it seemed. At Labrador Falls, I was to shoot first. It was a spectacular sight. The Churchill River plunged more than 200 feet into a narrow canyon, sending up a plume of mist that was visible against a rolling green carpet of sub-alpine firs from over 60 miles away. This was the picture I really wanted. A red-tailed, silvery gray F-102 in a 30-degree bank with the falls and mist behind it would be a calendar shot.

We flew over the falls at 500 feet to check the light through the mist. I selected my shot and dropped down to 200 feet. Minor was on my left. On the run-in, I locked the stick between my knees and readied my new Voigtlander. Through the viewfinder I could see Minor's jet perfectly positioned, at just the right distance. We were just about at the correct angle from the falls, so I pushed left with my knees to roll into a left bank.

Minor disappeared off the top of my viewfinder. Puzzled, I rolled out. He dropped past me like a rock, far too low for the picture, and way too close. Gradually, he came back into position. We were beyond the falls, but I thought I could salvage some sort of photo. I got Minor back in the viewfinder, then dropped the camera and grabbed the stick. He was thirty feet away—with his camera up to his eye!

We'd zoomed past that wonderful falls at 200 feet in formation, both of us flying with our knees, and a camera to our eye.

Minor's voice crackled in my helmet. "Chuck, what happened? That was pretty bad."

"Yeah, I know. Let's try it again. This time, you shoot. I'll be the model."

"I thought that's what we just did," he said.

"Well, sort of. How's your fuel?" I asked.

"Time to go home. We'll try it another day," he replied.

We never did. It would have been a great picture, though.

The crash of an HH-3 like this one started a chain of stressful events for the new commander.

Not Again

It's probably safe to say that the most exciting events in a fighter jock's life occur in the cockpit. However, that isn't universally true. The day I assumed command of the Pacific Life Support School (PLSS) was far more exciting than most days in the cockpit -- and it didn't let up nearly as quickly as a flying crisis.

I was fresh out of Vietnam, delighted to be in Okinawa with my family and happy to be trusted with my first command. We were responsible for training Air Force, Army and Marine aircrews in the skills that would help them survive an ejection or ditching at sea. We had eight boats, ranging from 31 to 84 feet long. Some belonged to the Air Force, some to the Army and one was owned by the Navy. Twenty-five airmen and non-commissioned officers made up the faculty and support staff. Each week a class of around sixty arrived for training in parachute landings at sea, dangerous marine life, rafts, signaling and helicopter pick-ups. We spent three days a week on the East China Sea in swim suits -- and best of all, our higher headquarters was 900 miles away in Fuchu, Japan. The only down side was that I had no fighter to fly.

I was assigned to fly a Korean War vintage T-33 jet trainer. That didn't seem too exciting. Since I had become non-current in physiological training while in the war zone, my first day on the job was scheduled to be in the physiological training classroom and their altitude chamber, getting reacquainted with the symptoms of hypoxia (lack of oxygen) at altitude. It seemed a rather bland way to begin.

While I was locked inside the iron and glass chamber my instructors would be taking about sixty students out onto the East China Sea to practice helicopter pick-ups. An Air Force HH-3 Jolly Green Giant was to lift them from the water with its hoist. It was a pretty safe operation, although the tremendous rotor wash and salt spray kicked up by the chopper tended to make it a bit hairy for the students. Two safety boats stood by to protect them from the hammerhead sharks that frequented the area and to retrieve them after the chopper crew put them back into the water after their pick-up. I wanted to be out there, but it was a "no sweat" situation. Or so it seemed.

Inside the chamber a dozen of us were going through a hypoxia demonstration at a pressure altitude of 35,000 feet. We each removed our oxygen mask and tried to determine our individual oxygen deprivation symptoms in time to put the mask back on before we passed out. I was getting a bit warm and fuzzy-headed when the instructor told me to put my mask on immediately. As soon as my head cleared up he handed me a phone. I took a couple of deep breaths, popped the mask loose again and answered, “Major Lehman speaking.”

“This is Chief Norberg. We’ve got a chopper down in the training area.”

“Did everyone get out OK?” I wasn’t too concerned, because the HH-3 was designed to float on its boat shaped bottom and the sponsons on each side.

“Yes, sir. We’ve got ‘em all in the boats - - but the chopper’s gone.”

“What do you mean, gone?” I asked.

“Sank, sir. It’s in about 310 feet of water. One of the instructors got a rope on it, though,” he replied. “It hit the water pretty hard. Probably ruptured the hull.”

Not a great way to start a job as a commander. I remembered my experience with an accident investigation board at Goose Bay (See “Out Of Here”, page 65) “No smart assed remarks this time,” I told myself. I thought a moment, then said, “OK, Chief, make sure they’ve got a good float on that rope, so we can recover the bird. Then get everyone back to the classroom. I’ll meet you there.

Oh yeah, the chopper crew may want transportation from our docks to their unit."

Back at PLSS I got a complete briefing from the Chief and several of the instructors. The chopper had picked up several students while in a low hover. They were on board while the hoist operator lifted another. The whole operation was enveloped in salt spray. Suddenly, both engines seemed to lose power and the chopper fell into the water. Both side doors were open. That was a mixed blessing. It allowed everyone to get out quickly - - but it also allowed water to get in quickly. Luckily, the huge rotors hit the water well away from the people swimming toward the safety boats, so no one was hurt.

That was the good news. The bad part was that we had a major accident on our hands, and it involved several major commands. Our school belonged to Pacific Air Force (PACAF). The chopper and crew belonged to Military Airlift Command (MAC). The students had come from the Army, Air Force and Marines. Clearly, this was one accident that was going to be scrutinized at the highest level in Washington.

Within twenty-four hours a full colonel from MAC arrived as accident board president. PACAF sent another colonel. The other members were a mixed bag. They immediately began taking testimony from all the witnesses.

My concern was that they would get the idea that somehow our training program was at fault.

Meanwhile, I contacted the army port at Naha to get help in recovering the helicopter. Within three days they had gotten a big seagoing tug with a huge crane to Okinawa. Their Okinawan divers went down to put a cable on the chopper. On the first lift the cable broke just as they were ready to lift the helicopter on board. A second dive and second lift went well, and we had physical evidence for the accident board. I was amazed at how much damage seawater could do to aircraft aluminum in just a few days. There was no way the bird would ever fly again.

Of course our student load did not let up during the investigation. We had sixty new aircrew members to train. That included academics, parachute drags, rafts, signaling, parasailing and helicopter pick-ups. For some reason the Air Force chopper unit wanted no part of us. They seemed convinced that the extended time they had to spend in a hover was too dangerous. I called the Navy unit on the island and they agreed to send an H-34 to pick up our students. It was an old chopper that could only handle six students at a time, so it would be a slow operation, but it would work. The students would have to jump out of the chopper after six had been picked up. That was no problem.

The morning of the exercise the accident board president called and asked to ride on the Navy chopper so he could see first hand how we trained. “Sure, Colonel. If it’s OK with the Navy, it’s fine with me. You can pick up your gear here,” I said with some misgivings. I jumped onto one of our safety boats and headed out about eight miles onto the East China Sea. The Navy bird arrived right on time.

I could see the colonel peering out the side door over the hoist operator’s shoulder. They picked up the first six students without incident. Just as the hoist operator swung the last one into the door, the engine made a strange sound - - and quit! The chopper fell like a rock, hitting the water about 75 feet from us with a huge splash. “Not another one,” I moaned. The crew managed to roll it just enough to smack the rotor blades into the water on the side away from us. They came unglued, but struck no one. Six students and the hoist operator - - followed by a wide-eyed colonel bailed out on our side as we moved in toward them. Only bubbles and an oil slick remained where the chopper had sunk. I watched anxiously for any sign of the crew. After what seemed like several minutes two white helmets popped to the surface. The pilots gasped for a moment, then broke into big smiles. We got everyone into the boats and headed for Okinawa. The colonel sat with his head in his hands, silent and shaking, after breaking at least one Olympic swimming record getting from the H-34 to our boat.

Less than a week on the job and two helicopters had slipped into fifty fathoms. As far as I knew, no survival or life support school had ever lost a chopper -- and we'd lost two in one week. It was *definitely* not a good way to begin a command.

Unlike the Air Force, the Navy did not seem too concerned about their loss. They had the crew back and that seemed to suffice. They didn't even want us to try to bring the chopper back up.

The president of the Air Force accident board was not too happy - - but his people cleared us of any fault in the loss of the HH-3. They determined that the crew had simply hovered too low. The rotors had kicked up enough salt spray to coat the engines' compressors with salt, messing up their airflow. That flamed out both engines.

We were certainly under a lot of watchful and skeptical eyes for the next year or so, but all went well, and the rest of our tour in Okinawa was great -- except for the decoy flight (next chapter).

ROCAF F-104's similar to these USAF versions were allegedly protecting me when I was an unwitting decoy.

Gombay Decoy

Not all combat missions are related to wartime -- and they're not always pre-announced.

The life support school job in Okinawa settled down just fine after its first hectic week. I enjoyed the job tremendously. Superb SCUBA diving was an added benefit. The whole family loved it. Flying the T-33 was OK, but the missions were less than exciting -- except for one.

I got a call one morning that I was to fly to Taiwan to act as a bogey for a Republic of China Air Force (ROCAF) air defense exercise. It sounded like a good break from the routine. Strangely, I was to go solo. Usually, both cockpits of the "T-Bird" were filled to provide training for two pilots. I assumed the reason for the solo trip was to save per diem funds. That was not the case.

I was told to pack a Mess Dress uniform, the Air Force equivalent of a tux. That seemed a bit strange.

The long overwater flight to Taipei was uneventful. I noticed that the bird seemed to run smoother over that warm water than it would have over the icebergs of Labrador or the ice floes of Lake Superior. There were five other USAF T-Birds on the ramp at Taipei. Each was from a different base, and each was flown by a single pilot. Strange.

We were put up in a fine hotel in town and reported to the ROCAF base early the next morning for briefing. We were each given an envelope instructing us to fly outbound from Taipei on generally westerly headings for a given number of minutes, then turn back in toward the island. We carried no chaff, there was to be no evasive action, no communication jamming and we were to maintain radio silence. Clearly, this was to be a pretty vanilla exercise -- not much of a challenge for the ROCAF Mach-two, F-104 fighters that would be intercepting us. Again, strange.

My packet called for an outbound heading of 276 degrees for 45 minutes at Angels 36, then a 180 degree turn to proceed back to Taipei at the same altitude and a reciprocal heading. The weather briefer told us in broken English that we would have a solid undercast at Angels five. I took off and began my climb to 36,000 feet. After leaving Departure Control frequency the radio was silent. I popped out of the clouds at five thousand, as advertised.

With no ground reference and no one to talk to, it was going to be a boring flight. The poor, under powered T-Bird struggled to 36,000 just before it was time to turn inbound. I knew that I was far out into the Straits of Formosa, but the only charts we had been given consisted of the navigational aids and air route structure of Taiwan, so I didn't know exactly where I was. As I began a gentle left turn to 096 degrees, there was a small hole in the clouds below me. Instead of blue water and sparkling whitecaps, I saw a brilliant green geometric pattern of RICE PADDIES!

It was Red China! I was probably, quite some distance into Chinese airspace. I was violating their sovereignty, and they were not likely to take kindly to that. I was in an unarmed trainer with no wingman to protect my six o'clock position (my tail). In Vietnam our squadron had lost an F-102 when a MIG popped up through the clouds and fired one missile, then dove back through the undercast before his wingman could do anything. If the Red Chinese decided to use that tactic to take me out, there was very little I could do. Suddenly, the whole mission made sense. I was a decoy! I wondered if our own Air Force knew that this was the ROCAF plan.

The T-Bird normally made a small radar target, but I was carrying a baggage pod that doubled as a radar reflector. To the Red Chinese radar operators, I looked like a large bomber. My only hope was that I was now heading outbound from their country, hopefully, looking fairly innocent.

I knew that both the Soviets and the Chinese had shot down aircraft they *claimed* were in their airspace. In my case, there was no doubt. My head was on a swivel. At the time, my eyesight was still 20/10 on a good day - - and I hoped this was one of them. At least I hoped to see the MIG's before they fired. Maybe I could out-maneuver them or their missiles. That was unlikely, given the T-Bird's stellar lack of performance at altitude. My mood alternated between fear and anger at being used. Possibly, the ROCAF F-104's were somewhere ahead of me over international waters, but close enough to engage the MIG's before they could get me. At least I hoped that was their plan. It was a long few minutes to "feet wet".

Once I was over the Straits, the ROCAF fighters showed themselves and ran several successful intercepts. I landed at Taipei still steaming.

There was no debriefing. Instead, we each received an invitation to a dinner that night at the ROC National Officers Club. The six of us caught taxis to the club. No one mentioned being over China. In my case, it was because I thought there was some possibility I had misread the time to my turn point. The others probably had not seen the ground. It seemed logical that we had been solo in those T-Birds so there would be no one to cross-check our target routes -- and no witnesses to where we turned. The ROCAF would have credible denial. It would be easier to blame any of us who got "caught." The whole operation began to make sense.

The club was magnificent. Nothing I had ever seen could compare to it. Opulent seems best to describe its architecture and decor. We were ushered into a beautiful dining room with six large round tables. Each was set for eight. There was more silver and crystal than I had ever seen. At least fifteen pieces of sterling flatware surrounded each splendid oriental plate. Five stemmed glasses stood beyond the plates. As if on cue, the room filled with three dozen general officers and colonels. With them were six junior officers. They escorted each of us Yanks to a different table, where we stood at attention facing a lieutenant or captain across the table. A brigadier general took his place on my left, while a colonel moved to the chair on my right. Four waiters stood at each table to pull out our chairs. All of the ROCAF officers were in their formal uniforms -- a full step above our mess dress.

We were barely seated when one of the lieutenants stood, raised his glass and said, "Gombay!" A single glass at each place had been charged with a pale liquid. Everyone raised that glass in toast, repeated the word

"Gombay" and drained their glass. My throat caught fire. My drinking consisted of an occasional glass of wine with dinner. The general on my left saw my discomfort and said in perfect English, "Would you rather have Pepsi?" I nodded, gasping. He motioned to one of the four waiters, and before the next toast my firewater had been replaced. The toasts went on all evening -- even after the lieutenant at our table slid off his chair onto the floor. He was ignored.

The dinner was beyond belief. Our impeccable waiters served *sixteen* courses with great pomp. Fifteen were superb. The only one that left me cold was chicken-foot soup. The bowl set in front of me was half full of a clear chicken broth with a naked chicken foot standing proudly in the middle. I ate the broth as properly as I knew how, then picked up the scaly, clawed foot. As I raised it to my mouth the general said, "Major, you don't have to eat that." I had no idea how I would have eaten it.

Our distinguished hosts were so gracious that I finally got the courage to mention my experience over Red China that morning. The general just smiled and said, "It was OK, major, my F-104's were ready to take over if the Peoples Republic tried anything. Too bad they didn't."

I didn't think it was too bad at all.

Apparently, the Red Chinese radar operators had been asleep that morning -- or maybe they'd been Gombaying the night before. If they had seen us, their government never let on. I decided to keep quiet about the whole deal. Since no international incident occurred, it seemed best to leave it that way.

Months later, when President Nixon visited Red China the US media broadcast a spectacular dinner that the communists put on for him. It was identical to the Gombay Dinner given by the Taiwanese for six innocent T-Bird drivers who had visited the Red China much earlier. I wonder if the President tried to eat his chicken foot.

Photo courtesy of Pat's World F106DeltaDart.com

Swan Song - The Last Flight

It's been said that the two worst things that can happen to a fighter pilot, are walking out to a fighter, knowing it will be your last flight, or walking out NOT knowing you will never again fly a fighter. I thought I had experienced the first of these in the early seventies, when I last flew the great F-106. My subsequent sorties were in the T-39 (military version of the Saberliner) hauling VIP's, and in the Cessna T-41 providing survival students the opportunity to practice vectoring rescue forces to their position. Both were pretty mundane. In fact, the T-39 experience taught me to begin drinking coffee. I found it very difficult to stay awake, boring holes through the sky with a load of distinguished persons on board. The coffee helped—but not much. Airline flying was not for me. People often asked why I didn't get out of the Air Force, and make some real money flying for the airlines. My standard response was that I felt it would be like stepping out of an Indy Car and into a Greyhound Bus.

In 1982, I found myself at Royal Air Force Alconbury, England as base commander of a three-base complex, hosting two flying wings and building facilities to host a ground launched cruise missile wing. One wing had RF-4 reconnaissance fighters and F-5's painted to look like Soviet aircraft. The F-5's were used to train NATO fighter pilots in combating Eastern Block tactics. The wing commander considered me a ground-pounder and never gave a thought to letting me fly—or even letting me fly *in* one of his two-place birds. That hurt!

For almost three years, I worked 80 or more hours per week, keeping things running as smoothly as possible for the flyers, but the burn to be back in a fighter cockpit did not fade. The job had some wonderful perks, however. Because of it, Marian and I were included in a lot of functions—or "Do's" as the Brits called them. There were receptions and parties with quite a few titled people, members of parliament and a couple members of the royal family. They were great people, and fun to be around. Most of the events included some officers of the Royal Air Force. One afternoon, I was standing near the food tables (where else) talking with a RAF Wing Commander —a fighter wing. He asked how I liked my job. I told him how I felt. His answer just about knocked me off my feet.

"That's no problem, Chuck. If they won't let you fly, come fly with us."

"You're joking," I replied, wondering where he'd been for almost three years.

"I would never joke about something like that. Just ring me up when you have a bit of time."

His wing flew the famous Harrier -- the "Jump Jet." There was no fighter in the world that I would have chosen ahead of it. The bird took off vertically, by vectoring the engine thrust downward through huge ducts in the fuselage. Once airborne, the thrust was gradually directed aft (to the rear) and the aircraft accelerated into normal flight. He told me their mission was low altitude. That was even better. I'd watched the Brits fly low altitude, and knew it meant skimming the treetops the way we often did in Labrador. This was too good to be true.

I had already put in my retirement papers, and had only a few weeks left in the Air Force, so I knew I'd have time for only one flight. As soon as we got everything set for our move back to the states, I called the Wing Commander. True to his word, he invited me to come right up to RAF Wittering.

His people checked me out in the Martin Baker ejection seat in the Harrier, and got me comfortable with the cockpit layout. The pilot who'd been honored by flying with me (would you believe *ordered* to take me under his wing) was an experienced Harrier jock. He immediately put me at ease, and said he'd handle the vertical takeoff, and begin the forward transition, then hand the bird off to me. That was OK. I'd heard how squirrelly the Harrier was while hovering. Our map of the mission showed a low altitude route that included RAF Alconbury. I had already told my deputy that if I had a chance, I would do my best to disrupt my own wing commander's staff meeting with a high-speed pass over the command post. I'd also asked him to make sure our commander knew why I was missing the staff meeting.

The RAF fighter jock lifted off smoothly, and I was struck by how weird it felt to be airborne in a fighter—which was not moving. He hovered for a few seconds, then dipped the nose in salute, turned in place and began to accelerate.

"You've got it, sir," he said.

I cannot imagine more beautiful music to a fighter pilot who's been out of the cockpit for several years. I took the stick and throttle. He gave me the bird at about 100 feet, so that's where we stayed, as we accelerated to 400 knots. It felt so good to be back at the controls of a high performance aircraft, that I had to bite my lip to avoid yelling something corny. We flew the assigned route until we were about ten miles from RAF Alconbury. I keyed the throttle-mounted mike button, and said, "Alconbury Tower, this is RAF 4736, ten miles West. Request a high-speed pass."

"Roger 736. You have no traffic. You are cleared for your pass. Say altitude."

"736 will be at 100 feet." We'd be almost that high, and there was no need to shake him up. "We'd like to stay slightly right of the runway." No need to mention the Command Post either.

Inside, at the staff meeting, the boss had just been told I was absent because I was flying the Harrier. My deputy said he just scowled and said nothing.

I shoved the throttle to the firewall, and accelerated to somewhere around 500 knots—although I wasn't looking at the airspeed. I was focused on the Command Post antennas. We missed 'em. I pulled up to a couple hundred feet and left the area. We got back on our flight plan, and landed at Wittering. I thanked my pilot and the commander profusely for a great close to a wonderful flying career.

As I walked back into my office at Alconbury, my deputy grinned broadly, and said, "You got him. He sure knew that wasn't one of his own birds. How close were you?"

"Close enough, I guess." Damn, that felt good!"

Radio Speak

To make radio transmissions easier to understand, and to make them shorter, we used a Brevity Code and the International Phonetic Alphabet. Here are some of the more commonly used terms. They appear in many of these stories.

ANGELS - Altitude in thousands of feet.
APPLEJACK - The highest state of readiness during an air defense exercise.
BANDIT - Enemy aircraft (real).
BIG BANG - A nuclear explosion.
BOGEY - Enemy aircraft (simulated).
BROKEN ARROW - A nuclear accident.
BUSTER - Use military power (full throttle without afterburner
CHICKS - Friendly fighters.
CONTACT - I have the bogey on my radar scope.
FIVE BY or **FIVE SQUARE** - Your transmission is loud and clear
GATE - Full power with afterburner.

HOME PLATE - The base where we were planning to land.

JUDY - I am taking over the intercept.

LEMON JUICE - The second highest state of readiness during an air defense exercise.

M. A. - Mission Accomplished.

M. I. - Missed Intercept

NO JOY - I have no radar or visual contact with the Bogey.

OVER - I am done with my transmission, and listening for your reply.

PIGEONS - The heading and distance to Home Plate or some other base.

PORT - Left turn or left side.

ROGER - I heard and understood your transmission.

RTB - Return to base.

SPLASH - The bandit is destroyed

STARBOARD - Right turn or right side.

TALLY HO or **TALLY** - I have visual contact with.....

VECTOR - Steer to this heading. i.e. Vector 270 (degrees)

WHAT STATE - How much fuel do you have? (In pounds)

ZULU - Greenwich mean time. The time in Greenwich, England.

International Phonetic Alphabet

A	Alpha	N	November
B	Beta	O	Oboe
C	Cocoa	P	Papa
D	Delta	Q	Quebec
E	Echo	R	Romeo
F	Foxtrot	S	Sierra
G	Golf	T	Tango
H	Hotel	U	Uniform
I	India	V	Victor
J	Juliet	W	Whiskey
K	Kilo	X	X-Ray
L	Lima	Y	Yankey
M	Metro	Z	Zulu

The author with the F-106. Note the optical sight at the apex of the windscreen.

Chuck and Marian Lehman in Puerto Vallarta, Mexico in 2006
Photo by Greg Lehman Photography

About the Author

Colonel Charles (Chuck) A. Lehman earned his Air Force commission and a degree in physics from St. Olaf College in Minnesota, his home state. He went to work for Westinghouse as a flight test engineer, while awaiting a pilot training slot. He earned his wings in 1958, and entered advanced training in the F-86L. He flew F-102's and F-106's with the 11th, 59th and 64th Fighter Interceptor Squadrons, 30th Air Division and Headquarters Air Defense Command accumulating about 3800 flying hours. Chuck has been married to his soulmate, Marian (Amundson) for more than 50 years. They have three children and nine grandchildren. Chuck and Marian live near Spokane, Washington.

Also by Colonel Chuck Lehman

EMERGENCY SURVIVAL
DESERT SURVIVAL HANDBOOK

These books are full of real-life stories that teach you how to handle common emergencies, whether you're in your car, boat or airplane, on skis,snowmobile or on foot. Learn from the mistakes of real survivors and from the things they did right.

ORDER FORM

Angels Three Six

By Colonel Chuck Lehman

(Please print)

Name: ______________________________

Address: ______________________________

City: __________________ State: ___ Zip: ________

Books by Chuck Lehman

Angels Three Six	$19.95 U.S. + $3.00 s/h
Emergency Survival	$9.95 U.S. + $3.00 s/h
Desert Survival Handbook	$7.95 U.S. + $3.00 s/h

(Includes state sales tax. For multiple purchases inquire for shipping discounts)

Enclosed is my check for the total amount of: _______

Make check payable to **CALCO**

Mail Check & Order Form to:

CALCO

13811 S. Finney St..

Medical Lake, WA 99022

Phone:(509) 299-7802

Email: cmlehman2@yahoo.com